Falling Into Place

A Brief History of New England

by

Thomas Jackson

RoseDog Books

PITTSBURGH, PENNSYLVANIA 15222

ISBN-10: 0-8059-7317-6
ISBN-13: 978-0-8059-7317-4
Library of Congress Control Number: 2006901953

Printed in the United States of America

First Printing

For more information or to order additional books,
please contact:
RoseDog Books
701 Smithfield Street
Third Floor
Pittsburgh, Pennsylvania 15222
U.S.A.
1-800-834-1803
www.rosedogbookstore.com

Eluwilussit allies with the Englishmen
John Pynchon and Benjamin Church

Medgedagik flees to Mayne
with his elderly grandfather,
Eluwilussit

Henri Adams and Machienthew
(changed to Mike Jartlow upon
enlistment) withstand many
hardships during their campaigns
in The War of 1812

Herbert finds Henri's
Journal in the foundation
of a burnt down barn
in Pittsfield

1500 A.D.   1900 A.D.

354 A.D.
Birth date of St. Augustine

1812-1814 A.D.
The War of 1812

1983 A.D.
The end of Jai
Alai for Pat

1675 A.D.
King Phillip's War

1637 A.D.
Pequot War

Timeline of Notable Events Discussed Throughout

"Falling Into Race"

Chapter 1
Jai Alai

In high school none of my energy was spent on academics, it was spent on something much more important. Even though I was able to graduate my passion lied in Jai Alai. I had perfect attendance despite doing none of my homework throughout the four years I attended Pittsfield High School. If it were not for my mother, Anna Adams, I would not have made it through. She embedded in me that wealth should not be determined by money. Wealth was so simple to achieve, yet impossible if I did not live by the truth. According to mother, happiness was only obtainable to those whose nature formed through the truth. My mother forced me to graduate, but my alcoholic father instilled that the truth was eternal.

My knowledge was from far more than one just influence. My mother's was the most important; she was the only one who told me go to school everyday. She said, school was the only opportunity I had at learning what human nature really was, within the knowledge of the past. However, I achieved most of my education through my ancestors' experience, not schoolwork.

My father, Russell, had a different opinion as to my mother's. His thoughts were based on his predisposed disadvantage.

He said to me once, "I have no opportunity for success because I have no chance at making money." My older brother, Mark, was affected most by Russell's anecdotes. Dad felt that the only opportunity his two strongly built American Indian sons had at obtaining wealth was either through athletics or agriculture.

His opinion of my high school education was that it hid the immorality of the foundation that democracy was built upon. My father dropped out of school, just as my troubled brother, Mark, had. They both did not believe that school would help them gain financial wealth. Mainly, the past lives of our American Indian descendants reminded my father of the inevitable injustice that could not be denied. However, my father's knowledge of the justice the original New England natives received greatly influenced my nature. Consequently, I could not accept my wealth until his death.

If it were not for my mother's advice, I would have fallen into place as my father and brother, who both dropped out of school because of drugs. My father also felt farming was more important for his American Indian sons' than a misleading public school. I became convinced that I could not succeed as a scholar, all because of my father's drunken negativity.

My only concern in life had become the sport I fell in love with, because of my loving grandfather. As soon as my mother's father, Jacques, introduced it to me, I never wanted to stop. He taught Jai Alai to me in only two hours, while we were playing against the wall of his Berkshire estate. Unfortunately for my whole family, my father had an angry meltdown about life when he saw me playing with my grandfather, and went off about Anna and Jacques as a French family. Russell told me I could not play the Basque game any longer, with or without my grandfather. For a brief period, I was never able to play because my father "supposedly" burnt the sticks. He broke both my grandfather Jacques' and my own heart due to his hatred of any

European power. He told me he did not accept his son participating in Grandfather Jacques' Basque culture.

Contrary to my father's opinion, I knew Jai Alai was my only calling. When I was six Grandpa Jacques Dubois, who became a phenomenal player through his relatives, spent his free time teaching me the game. My mother's family, the Dubois family, reached America around the time of the Revolutionary War from France. Jacques' descendants brought Jai Alai, which originated from the Basque culture. Grandpa Jacques' descendants first arrived after the revolution in the open land of Maine, which was part of Massachusetts at the time. Immediately after Maine became a state and was no longer a province of Massachusetts, the Dubois family moved to Ohio in 1820. Eventually, Grandpa Jacques moved his family and Basque culture, from Ohio to Pittsfield, attempting to spread its popularity. Yet, only his cooking made an impact on the people of Pittsfield beginning in the 1950's.

In Pittsfield, the expansion of Jai Alai, Jacques' main passion, only influenced one. Unfortunately, my father, his only son in law, turned him off to sharing his passion with others in Pittsfield, except for myself. It was nothing new for my father as every time he got drunk, he released his hatred of the expanded debauchery. His negative disposition caused Jacques to think twice about his ancestor's past.

Ironically, the only potential I inherited from my family was Grandfather Jacques' Jai Alai ability. When I was a kid, all I wanted was to be just like my rich French grandfather, and not a farmer as my father. Because of Grandpa Jacques, I focused all mind, body, and spirit on Jai Alai, instead of becoming an alcoholic Native American. Becoming a professional player in the developing American game was a dream for me throughout adolescence, yet my father could not accept that.

As my love for Jai Alai strengthened with the love for my grandfather, my father got jealous. Unfortunately, I never touched a stick again, after the brief two year introduction by Jacques. The only reason that my father took away the game I loved was because of his hatred for life. In Russell's opinion, the French had been just as responsible for The War of 1812 as the English.

A year before Grandpa Jacques died in 1973 he gave his cherished sticks to my mother to hide in the trunk of the green family station wagon before leaving his Berkshire mansion. The plan, between my mother and grandfather, was for Anna to give them to me to practice with once we arrived back to our farm. He knew I had finally found something I loved, even though my father hated it. Unfortunately, once we arrived back in Pittsfield after the day with Grandpa Jacques, Russell found the sticks I was about to practice with, and said, "I am going to burn them to ashes." My father wanted no affiliation with jai alai.

The destruction of the sticks was true, until the one summer night months following the arson. As soon as I was done working on the farm, my athletic older brother, Mark, revealed to me that our father had not burnt the sticks. He told me that he found them in the attic of the "haunted barn" that our other grandfather, Herbert, rebuilt on our farmland in Pittsfield. Mark had no fear of the barn after discovering the real reasons our father entered it and told us it was haunted. After Mark's discovery, he then began to join our father inside the barn.

It had been haunted, according to our Grandfather, Herbert, since 1856. It became haunted, according to Grandpa Herbert's story, when the original barn was burnt with Henri Adams in it to quarantine the disease that killed him. My Grandfather Herbert discovered the experiences of many of our descendant's from the journal he found that was stored and hidden in the foundation of the same burnt barn that Henri was burnt in. When Herbert found Henri's journal, he figured it was stored there from a past Adams. The unknown descendent put the journal in a fireproof safe in the basement of Henri's

4

barn right before it was burnt. The barn, even though burnt down to the foundation, had linked Herbert to all the spirits from the journal that Henri had shared. Grandfather Herbert had felt Henri's spirit every night in the barn he rebuilt. Herbert told his grandsons and son, Russell, that the spirits were good. Yet, Russell still did not let his children enter it because of the "evil demons inside."

The barn had been very good to Grandpa Herbert. Buried under debris, was where he had found the journal of Henri's that motivated him to discover historical truths. While digging up the foundation for a new barn to replace the burnt one with Henri's dead body in it, he discovered the journal in a miniature fire safe vault. If Grandpa Herbert had never found the journal, he would not have attempted the research as he had, and ultimately answer so many questions for himself and his fellow Native American descendents.

At first, Mark became very paranoid from the ghost stories he heard while inside the barn with our father. He shut off from the world around him and began hearing outside voices within. He never wanted to know anything about his descendant's war experiences, which were all written in the journal. Instead, Mark had his mind on the same empty evil, which was also apparently in the barn. Russell told his eldest son that Henri's ghost always whispered in his ear, as he hallucinated in the barn, "you have no chance Russell." However, Mark lost all fear of the barn after discovering the agriculture that our father hid within it.

One late summer night after working on the farm, Mark told me, his timid younger brother, that he found Grandpa's Jai Alai equipment that our father supposedly burnt. Apparently, he snuck into the barn without our father knowing. He climbed up into the attic and found Grandpa Jacques' sticks. He whispered to me, "dad knew I knew."

I did not believe my wacky brother at first, because our father always told us that he had burnt Grandpa Jacques' sticks. Even with the assurance of Mark that the sticks were in the attic, I still argued that he should not break our father's rules, and should never go in the haunted barn alone. I screamed at my brother, "Dad said the sticks were not to be used ever again".

My obedience had no effect on Mark. Almost immediately after my stern objection, he then went on to tell me about how he hung out in the barn with Dad all the time, but he would not tell me what they did. Mark claimed, "If the sticks were really not burnt and placed in the attic of the abandoned barn, Dad obviously wanted them to be used again." However, I still felt that they were never to be used again, as our father wanted no affiliation with the western culture, which devastated and stole the Indian's peaceful culture.

A big part of me needed to know if the sticks were really there. Perhaps it came from the love of my grandfather within, or perhaps it was because, ever since my father took away the sticks, every day was filled with thoughts about playing Jai Alai again. To prove me wrong Mark decided to go up in the attic and get the sticks himself. However, he knew he wasn't going alone, I was close behind him. As I followed Mark up into the attic, I popped my head up, and not only found the Jai Alai sticks Mark had mentioned, but also some American Indian wardrobes of past Adams descendants.

I was very nervous and stayed away from everything; because in the back of my head I sensed that Dad knew of our disobedience. Mark picked up a stick and handed it to me while I was distancing myself in the corner. He then said, "Let's play."

Climaxing with that moment, I became very excited. I forgot about my father and his uncontrollable anger for the ten minutes that I played outside. However, I was reassured of my intuition once he looked out the window and witnessed his sons experiencing the most fun that they'd ever had. As I whipped the ball off the barn, he sprinted out of the house with a beer in his hand and a look of disgust on his face.

My father eventually told me that I could keep the sticks, but unfortunately it came after he had first punched me and then said, "The only reason Jai Alai is becoming popular in America is because it involves gambling, you idiot. Don't you see boy, the only thing in our society that brings happiness is money and we'll never have any. Even if you think you can get rich by this sport, there is another man greedier than yourself that will take your dirty money because of your errant behavior."

After that night, I didn't care for anything my father ever said again. I completely ignored the alcoholic for the first time in my fourteen years. After getting punched, the advice that Grandpa Jacques had told me about my father finally clicked. He told me, after my father apparently burned the sticks, to never listen to another word out of my drunken father's mouth. However, my grandfather was only reassuring me of what I had come to realize. My father's negative opinion of Jai Alai, and the underground pressures of money that he always spoke of was no concern of mine, and even though I knew he would never listen, I would always assure my father that the gambling and gangster stories of Jai Alai were all farces.

Mainly, I hated dealing with my father, because he was always drunk. Yet, I made it seem as though I had a change of heart the moment Jai Alai was finally accepted. I knew my father could do nothing about his uncontrollable temper and violent behavior, and came to terms with what I could not change as long as I could play the game I loved. As a result of our disobedience, I was left with only a bloody nose. Mark, on the other hand, got the bruising. He was the one that came up with the idea, which defied our father. Furthermore, he had actually promised our father that he would never show me the sticks. After Dad punched me, he picked up a stick, and feeling sorry for his bleeding thirteen year old, handed it over. He left me there while he paced in the barn, holding it for ten minutes, before he finally, to my surprise, said, "You can use them, but only after work."

Leaving me with that, he then brought Mark into the barn and shut the door behind him. After that beating Mark was never the same again. His pride had been beaten out of him. He no longer felt worthy, enough for even his own family, and distanced himself from that point forward. The damage was permanent, and after my father put Mark through four hours of torture, he was forced to find comfort in something other than his family.

After it took almost a week for Mark to recover, he tried playing a game of Jai Alai for the first time. He couldn't understand the game at first because he had never tried it before with Grandpa Jacques. After I explained all the principles that Grandpa taught me, my brother and I became a solid pair. Luckily for our newly found recreation, our father was too busy at the bar, arguing politics, to condemn the sport he hated so much. Or perhaps the guilt our father felt after beating out our innocence prevented him from taking anything further.

Unlike my father and his alcoholic escape, I found a different outlet for my stress. Every night after work I would play against the barn wall for hours on end, regardless of my drunken father's relentless cursing. In Massachusetts the sport was extinct, but not for me. I spent every bit of my free time playing, some of the time with my older brother, against the same Pittsfield barn Grandpa Herbert rebuilt. After my astonishing reencounter with Jai Alai, I surprised even myself with my skill. Mark became very jealous of my ability. He had lost all opportunity with athletics after becoming expelled the senior year of his highly anticipated basketball season. Unfortunately for Mark, father had never told him that what they did inside the walls of the barn needed to stay inside the walls of the barn. Mark never should have smoked in front of others.

Luckily for Mark, our mother was a very tolerant woman. After his expulsion, and Russell's nightly escape with alcohol, she was still able to continue living with and loving the men that she called family. She moved to Pittsfield from Ohio with her parents, who had been gypsies. Anna's father had a love for cooking, and her mother for teaching. Anna, it seemed, shared this love of her mother's, as she later also became a teacher in order to support her own family. The Dubois' were disturbed by the destruction of Ohio's open land and couldn't bear to witness it any further. They had lived in a trailer on thirty acres of land that was never touched, until shortly after they moved.

On one hand in Ohio, eminent domain took from Anna's parents, fifteen acres of land for industrial purposes. Pittsfield's land, on the other hand, had an untouched purity that Jacques felt, or hoped, would never be destroyed. He shared the same love for nature, as his daughter had. His lost rights of territory had also paralleled his descendants, who in 1820 left Maine after their land became claimed by the independent state of Maine.

When Grandpa Jacques arrived with his family in Pittsfield he did not have a job. However, he did receive a substantial amount of money for his claimed property in Ohio. He combined his cooking skills with a portion of this unfortunate fortune and began a restaurant that later brought him hundreds of thousands of dollars. Jacques gained great success in Pittsfield due to his French restaurant. He had inherited both culinary and athletic abilities from his French ancestry, making him excel in two areas, French cooking and Jai Alai.

During her teenage years, Anna had worked as a waitress at the restaurant her father owned. It was there where she met the man who first introduced himself as "the chief" in 1959. While Russell was eating at Bon France with his father, Herbert, he met the women he would later love, and hit, like no other. After noticing Anna's beautiful eyes, Russell tried grabbing her attention by telling one corny joke after another. Soon enough his attempts at flirtation worked, and the next time he ate at the restaurant he left with Anna's home address in his pocket. On their first date the two enjoyed drinking together and disagreeing with the political system, it was a match made in heaven. Eight months later they married, and ironically seven months after the wedding Anna gave birth to their first son, Mark. Unfortunately, it wasn't until after Mark's birth that Anna decided to say goodbye to the lifestyle that had since then delegated her and her husband's life together. After seeing the effects that alcohol had on her newborn son, Anna's guilt drove her into abstinence. When alcohol left Anna's bloodstream, Russell left her heart.

Consequently, after Anna quit drinking, her relationship with Russell changed drastically. The communication that had always come so easy between them turned into a chore. Somewhere after her extensive binge, Anna, it seemed, had lost the ability to share her feelings, something so easy for her to do when she was drunk. However, where Anna struggled with emotions, Russell lacked them completely. Unless drunk or stoned, he was unable to express his emotional position. His dependency blinded him from seeing the real damage that alcohol was having on his life. He had no problem ignoring his pregnant wife's damaging acts, as she would match him shot after shot in each of her three trimesters. Just like his father in law, Russell also seemed to inherit a few traits from his ancestors. His mother died from liver complications of alcoholism.

For Anna, alcohol was never used again after Mark's pregnancy. My brother had suffered mild birth defects from alcohol in the womb. Fortunately, the two were able to strengthen him into a physically healthy baby. On one hand, the entire experience did not change Russell's nature. Anna, on the other hand, could not bear to drink another drop of the substance that altered her baby. Lucky for me, I was the next and final Adams born between Anna and Chief Russell.

After discovering how careless Anna had behaved during her pregnancy, Jacques lost all positive emotion towards her. Before the birth of Mark, with the success of their restaurant in Pittsfield, they were able to live the "Anglo Monarchic Aristocratic"[i] way of life. By owning such a restaurant in Town Square, Jacques felt his family had finally found success. He took great pride in the restaurant, and his daughter. The two brought Jacques infinite happiness, or so he thought. The success of his restaurant brought no happiness to him after he knew what Anna had done to her first born.

My other grandfather, Herbert, was also affected by the careless acts of his son and daughter-in law. He, too, felt a loss of wealth after witnessing what Anna and Russell had done. The event seemed to be a catalyst of depression. One afternoon while Jacques and Herbert were speaking together, Herbert told Jacques that there was no longer any proper way of life in their society, because it was built on a fractured foundation. Herbert learned a lot from Henri's historical journal, and it ignited his extensive research on the first civil war in New England. He discussed the King Phillip's War along with The War of 1812 with Jacques and his son, Russell, almost every time the three were together.

After listening to the wisdom of Herbert, Jacques had assured him that as unfortunate as the past exterminations had been, none of us could have prevented them. Herbert agreed and told Jacques that his and Russell's society, like many past, will always differ in opinion of justice, because the powerful did not divide prosperity.

My father agreed, and before his death, he expressed all his manifestations of wrong to me. He told me all he knew on the past acts of immoral nature discussed by his elders. Mainly, Russell gained his opinion of immorality after reading the journal, which described Henri's and other ancestors past experiences. Unfortunately, Grandfather Herbert would not discuss excerpts of the journal with me.

My father's anger, in contrast, grew from the knowledge he obtained from Henri's journal. Every story of Henri's my father had described to me was about wars that destroyed many Native American tribes; I negatively absorbed it all. My inherited negativity and sheltered lifestyle left little room for anything positive, except Jai Alai. Luckily for Mark and me, our Grandfathers and mother differed from my father. They felt obligated to pass on good nature toward us, unlike the bitter Russell. However, Mark ignored their attempts at teaching good. He unfortunately only seemed to be influenced by Russell and his negative justifications. This negativity ultimately drove Mark into the same dependency of deviancy as our father. My mother, Anna, just couldn't get through to Mark. She couldn't make him realize the importance of true wealth. Instead, Mark shared the same interpretation of wealth as my father, that it was a material.

Russell saw wealth as impossible. According to him, it was impossible for minorities who could only work the petty jobs available to them. He felt that the hardest workers only supported the wealthy. The richest and most powerful men in the past had only achieved economic dominance through slavery. My father always went on about how the petty worker attempted to gain worth through positive effort, yet the effort only became minimally rewarding through facilitating the wealthy to enhance, or remain balanced. He felt that money had become extinct to Native Americans. The destructive expansion that began in New England only rewarded Native Americans for killing or being deceitful to fellow natives. From the seventeenth to the twentieth century, the only option for those who were underprivileged of receiving wealth was gained by performing acts for the wealthy.

However, because of my Grandfather Herbert's influence, I assumed that everyone was equal. He first taught me that democracy was only one voice, unified to establish freedom through a partnership of equality. He then made me realize that our people never had an equal chance at happiness. He also instilled in me that no man was greater than the other, based on physical appearance. Forcing a war based on expansion of debt to other cultures is no democratic act. He said, "Men should be judged for their actions towards others, not for words."

Yet, according to my father's theory, the structure of democracy was formed upon the destructive expansion of universal justice. Russell felt the past had defeated any chance at true Freedom for Native Americans. He once asked me, how is it possible for a man to develop properly without any successful example to learn from? I had no answer, because I knew that with the molding of the American foundation, many men that were dependable workers (slaves) were also considered as aboriginal savage. My father strongly felt that the past injustices did not allow for any creed of American to receive equality.

Grandfather Herbert disagreed with his son, that men of minority had minimal opportunity for success. He told me, "Life's greatest success should be simply teaching and learning from others."

Our father, however, always reminded my brother and me that equality, and success, had been eliminated through manufacturing of the predetermined. Through sacrifices of the poor, those predetermined into dominance created an ever-expanding gluttony by the dominating party.

The writings within the journal created most of my father's assumptions. They led him to believe that authority of rule validated all prior damaging acts by public servants toward fellow countrymen. My father attempted to prove this point to me by telling me about the journal and Henri's writings within it.

He told me that while fighting in The War of 1812, Henri had written how the governing body of America attempted to destroy New England's commerce and militia. I learned that the embargo, which the Republican Party put on all foreign trade, crippled New England before the war. However, with the same knowledge, Grandpa Herbert did not share the same feeling as his son. He was much older and wiser than my father would ever be. He knew that there was good and bad in everything and it would be impossible for every leader to be just. As a result, equal opportunity would be forever unattainable because of these corrupt men.

I learned that those virtuous members of the Federalist Party, who had stood for peace and honesty in our evolving nation, were lost with The War of 1812. In their place, the Republican Party had formed, led by the Virginians, Jefferson and Madison, his secretary of state, uniting the Non Federalists and many wicked Federalists. All these politicians favored an expanding government based on individual reward. At first, the Non Federalist Party did not gain majority because of its pessimistic name. However, this party, as a whole, later formed through Democrats and Republicans and manipulated the constitutional ethic of the Federalist Party.

My father would always go on drunken rampages explaining how I was doomed, because the ruler in a democracy has the ability to be nothing but a tyrant. He told me that it was impossible for a ruler to please everyone in a democracy. The poor must be hurt with injustice to benefit the privileged with justice. This was demonstrated throughout New England's formation, which Henri also wrote about throughout his journal, and reflected on it as far back as Henri's great great grandfather, Eluwilussit, beginning in Springfield (1674).

Through the journal, Russell learned that the expansion of control conquered profitable land from the original natives of New England during King Phillip's War in 1675. The invincible English force later attempted to conquer land, such as the St. Lawrence River, from the inhabitants and colonists during The War of 1812.

In the journal, Henri not only described his own experiences in battle during The War of 1812, but also those of his great great grandfather, Eluwilussit, in King Phillip's War. Eluwilussit had played a momentous role in the civil war of King Phillip. My father read that Eluwilussit had withstood the same devastating expansion in the King Phillip's War as Henri had in The War of 1812. The strife occurring to the New England Indians during their inevitable defeat in King Phillip's also happened to New Englanders during The War of 1812. In both wars no one man had control of his own destiny. The English force had the ability to destroy anything.

Russell assumed, through his father's discovery and research, that the King Phillip's War and The War of 1812 both had used bureaucracy over inhabitants to gain monarchial control. The crown took advantage of an unstable and unprepared nation who had declared war upon its mother in 1812, mainly because the Con Federalists were rewarded as President Madison defied tranquility by declaring the war and seizing control over the state's militia. My father compared the two wars as he read the journal and realized that at certain points war is inevitable, as long as party, not national, interest rein supremacy.

My father also taught me how the control was established amongst English settlers during King Phillip's "civil war"[ii] of New England in 1675. Freedom only became achieved through colonial justice. Unfortunately for the original inhabitants of New England, this freedom was only granted to the English. Consequently, the rulers demonstrating the destructive expansion during King Phillip's War had shared their philosophy with enlightened beneficiaries. Unfortunately, this evolution of violence forced separation amongst Americans during The War of 1812.

Russell had no respect for the past administration in 1812 whose acts forced his Native American brethren into countless unnecessary battles, none of which benefited the sacrificing soldiers. My father always used the example he learned from his father on the Battle of New Orleans. He told me that the battle benefited America greatly. Not only did the battle that happened after the end of The War of 1812, rid the state of unwanted inhabitants, it also gave America a favorable victory over the English, which strengthened the south's moral. This victory made him question the society, which created gluttony as the only means to define wealth. Yet, somehow everyone was still considered equal.

Russell, drunkenly crusaded all of his knowledge to me, used the journal as a definitive source to unlock knowledge. Russell claimed that colonial rule continued committing destructive acts before and after King Phillip's (Civil) War to gain control. This colonial force strengthened through its alliance with Indian tribes, who fought and located other Indians. He knew this because our very own descendant, Eluwilussit, was one of the Indians who turned his back on his Indian brothers for alliance with the English.

The extermination of Native Americans separated the tranquil men from the selfish men, and somehow the assumption that all men had the same opportunity for freedom in America was formed during and after these malicious acts. Those questioning the justice of expansion were considered to be evil. The rebellious Indian's in Phillips War and the Federalist's in 1812, were both threatened with treason for disagreeing with immoral acts valid only by God's will to expand. Unfortunately, for the Native Americans in King Phillip's War, they were not viewed under the same creed, even if they were a practicing Christian, in which God's will justified all the acts of genocide through violence against infidels. Praying natives were incapable to gain equal worth, yet were still able to fight for their colony. "For unchristianized natives there was only Anglo Saxon justice interpreted by the redmen as contempt[iii]

Russell assumed that gaining reign through God, sometimes not morally, became one of the principal practices of past rulers to successfully obtain both wealth and power. When my father finished reading Henri's journal, he pondered why his father would not let him illegitimately gain success, just as rulers had relied on during both of the wars mainly mentioned in the journal. Russell once quoted the journal to me on the subject, "In retrospect the government of Massachusetts ascribed King Phillip's War to God's indignation over the sins of the people who had become lax in church discipline, had forgotten to train their children alright, and had forsaken the paths of their fathers and had permitted their women to expose their bosoms, to dress their hair indecently and to wear too many ribbons.

However, Grandpa Herbert "ascribed it more nearly to application of Puritan Ideas of department and government to proud and sensitive Indians who had not been made instruments of aid as in Connecticut"[iv]

Maybe that is why my father never could define his worth, which according to him was obsolete. He blamed the system in which opportunity was only achievable for the few able to be guided by the cruel nature expansion brought. The kind and honest were unable to bridge the gap, which formed from immoral acts, and failed, based on the misconception that only legitimacy can build success.

Foreign power throughout the two unnecessary wars had initiated the deviant propaganda amongst savage Indians and then later the colonists. The wars of injustice broadened the importance of fighting imperative wars to gain control. The crown may have lost men from battles, yet they had set up a system in which they had total control of men who were from a financially thriving country.

The inhabitant's life during war became a source of profit for the conquerors. The powerful had been enlightened, so their expansion from first to last conquer would continue the irreversible destruction. The only option to gain wealth for inhabitants of a conquered frontier, according to my father, Russell, was obtaining power by controlling through immorality.

As both inner and financial wealth had avoided Russell, it was impossible to show his children something he could not obtain. The farm, which he spent his entire life on, looked as if it had been deserted the five years following my Grandfather Herbert's death. The only reason that the farm's lawn was ever mowed was because of me. As for our father, Mark and I were very lethargic. Luckily, I broke through and graduated high school.

For me, but especially Mark, staying in and studying for a higher education was impossible. Our father's disagreement with every institution of his sons' generation gave no concern for education. The only important things he had us concentrate on were to maintain the farm and perform well in high school sports.

Our father had set up a basketball hoop on the east side of the barn when Mark was three. It remained hanging the day we left. It got little wear after Mark's expulsion. Basketball was never my interest though I played my freshman year. Jai Alai remained in my heart. It seemed that my father did not care if I quit basketball; the only concern of his was getting drunk. I asked him when I graduated to quit. I told him, "I will never talk to you again if you are drunk tomorrow Dad."

He did not care how I felt and the next week he fell into place.

Before he died, my father felt his eldest had the most potential towards success. Russell felt that Mark's only opportunity at wealth was through basketball, because he averaged twenty points a game his junior year. Unfortunately for Mark, he did not listen to what Grandpa Herbert shared with us about playing sports. For many without lessons of life, athletics over academics became a fun, more realistic alternative for success. Yet, athletics only builds success for the few who fight through struggle, and without any example of success the effort becomes useless.

I, however, played Jai Alai everyday while I was finishing up with high school. As I began playing again, my virtues began to change from my father's assumptions. Luckily, I improved my academic results sophomore year once my teacher, Ms. Foley, sat me down. She told me that she did not want me to get kicked out of school as my older brother and that I should not listen to my father. Once I found out what my teacher's expectations were, I passed my final courses in high school. I only earned an academic presence in school because I bullshitted both my Grandfather Herbert and father's historical theories of the Indian's devolution throughout the two wars. My teachers understood because it seemed to be the only thing discussed in our family. Mainly, all my teachers felt sorry for my situation.

The entire high school knew the Adams experience. Mark was known for getting kicked off the basketball team and my father was known as the town drunk, drug dealer, and historian. Mark had become mainly known for what he did to get kicked off the team, not what great things he did on it.

The Pittsfield High School basketball fans at Mark's games were always enthralled with my father's comments in the stands. It seemed as if he got into a shouting match with just about anyone every game. It was so bad for me while I played on the freshman basketball team that I had to quit.

Mark, however, attempted many sports in high school, only because our father continually reinforced our ancestor's superior abilities. Mark was average in soccer but was a star for the basketball team, up until his mental disorder became the scapegoat for his deviance.

Coach Gilbert, his basketball coach, had Mark expelled his senior season after getting caught smoking some of his father's farm grown pot in a hotel room on an overnight trip. After the incident, Mark dropped out of school entirely and chose the same destructive destiny as our father. Both had fallen into the same spiral as most dropouts.

I tried out for the freshman basketball team following my older brother's success. Not only had my father's drunken rants made me quit, but I also could not make a lay up. I became mortified every time I had a breakaway. I did not understand the most important element of basketball, putting it in the hoop. Those were the main reasons why when I picked up the sticks and never wanted to put them down. I became addicted to Jai Alai. It was the first sport that I was better than my older brother in. What once was my brother's backboard became my wall.

For me, to have any success with Jai Alai in Massachusetts was impossible, yet I was still content with only playing at night and making only five dollars a day working on the farm throughout high school. Unfortunately, I had to pick up the slack of my drunken father and stoned brother.

And making matters worse, Chief Russell somehow correlated the corruption of past rulers with the game of Jai Alai. He felt that both had become greatly successful through illegitimacy. Simply, the imported Basque game, which he felt the Indians help broaden through other games, somehow reminded the chief of the Native American struggle for equality.

Chief Russell did not ever want his sons to deal with the same circumstances that our native ancestors and he had faced. Russell was mocked in school for his overwhelming knowledge of endangerment toward Native Americans. Other children in school called him the red chief everyday before he dropped out in the seventh grade. He, however, still kept half the nickname, and that is how he inheritably became known as the chief, unlike my Grandfather Herbert's legitimate acknowledgement.

Chapter 2

Suicide

The anger of my father, mixed together with a bottle of brandy, came out on me in 1979 during his final week of life.

It all began at my graduation party. My father, known as the chief by everyone else, arrived home late, as the bar was more important to him than his graduated son. When he stumbled into the party, fashionably late, he saw me wearing one of the family's headdresses I was never supposed to touch. The heirloom was stored in the barn attic to keep its authenticity. To make matters worst, I was holding a Jai Alai stick. I made matters even worse, because after I saw my father arrive I instantly began to imitate him, wobbling back and forth in front of my guests. I had no problem showing what little friends I had the respect I had for the drunk. Unfortunately for me, Chief Russell made a drunken mockery out of me, embarrassing me for life.

"Take off that shit, you ain't no Indian boy. You think you graduate and know everything, you ain't shit Pat," screamed my father in my disgraced face.

I then screamed, "Fuck you loser," in front of everyone.

Next thing I knew, the chief punched me at my own graduation party.

After a black eye and a lot of tears, Anna consoled me inside the house. However within the fifteen minutes everyone left, the chief followed his distraught wife and nose bleeding son inside. That's when he told me, "My youngest son is worthless and won't become anything if he continues to defy his father's rule."

Yet again, Anna attempted to kick the chief out, for good. This time, though, he left accordingly after he saw me bleeding and crying. My mother tried her hardest to keep my spirits high. It worked after she ended up telling me the only way I have succeeded thus far is through the unwillingness of our ancestors to quit, they never let any man's word or actions weaken their effort toward true freedom. "It was [Henri's] glory to bear the most horrible tortures without a sign of sufferings".

After punching me, the chief once again found his way to the local bar, leaving his distraught family, except this night he ended up passed out in the quiet back ally, and not with Anna. The chief attempted to sober up, after getting thrown out because of his disgustingly drunken act. He got a hotel room, and finally found the nerve to call Anna after a week of silence and sobriety. When Russell called, my mother threatened to change the locks on all the doors and never let the boys speak to him if he was ever drunk around us again. After that phone call the chief immediately began thinking of life without his family. He was an alcoholic and only knew how to handle his problems by drowning them. Within an hour after the phone call he was drinking again. The thought of losing his sons was too frightening to bear while sober. After half a handle of vodka, however, the chief's fear turned into fury. He was ready to face his problem, and in a drunken stupor he headed back to the farm.

The drunk chief stepped foot on our Pittsfield estate, after a three mile walk of contemplation, and did not realize that he was about to make his last visit. When he walked into his bedroom it was just about 10:00 PM and Anna was already in bed. "Anna," he screamed.

Instantly, she jumped out of bed expecting to see a sober husband. Undoubtedly, she thought he would change, considering her ultimatum. She walked towards her husband with every intention of kissing him. However, once she smelt his breathe, she slapped him instead, screaming, "How dare you."

The chief felt a need to justify the slap. Almost instinctively he punched his wife in the nose. As I watched from the steps above, it felt like deja vu, recalling my own bloody nose from my father's fist. After seeing his two sons looking down upon him with disgust, and blood pouring from his wife's nose, he ran out the door. After checking our mother with Mark, I sprinted out the door after my father into the Pittsfield woods. Mark stayed with our mother to stop the bleeding.

My father could not gather his actions. He seemed to be hallucinating while sprinting through the woods he knew entirely. I don't think he knew why he was running but continued the descent due to confusion. As I sprinted after my father I had one intention. I increased with speed with every inch I gained on the wobbly drunk, my anger motivated me into an impossible speed. Once I reached the cliff at the end of the woods overlooking the cemetery, I stopped. I could no longer hear my father. When I looked down upon the cemetery, I saw only the dark hundred foot descent to the burial ground. I wondered where Dad was hiding when I heard Mark's voice begin to approach from behind a flashlight. "Where's Dad?" cried Mark.

"I don't know," I said grimly. "He finally may have fallen into place." I then snagged the flashlight, and slowly began to shine its light down the hundred foot cliff. As the light reached the cemetery, filled with three hundred plots, Mark noticed our father's limp body. As fast as we could, we ran down the side of the cliff to our father's side. After realizing the chief's condition, we panicked. Looking back and forth at one another we couldn't speak for at least five minutes.

Suddenly the words, "No man has flown greater than your father," came out of the chief's mouth. Somehow he had survived the ninety foot fall. However, only moments later the chief was dead.

"He has no pulse," advised my calm brother, Mark. "We need to stop the bleeding and get Dad back to the house." My brother and I then carried our father's bloody limp body up the cliff and a mile to the farm. We finally arrived home to a teary eyed sympathetic mother.

She started screaming once she saw the blue chief, "It's all my fault. I shouldn't have slapped him. I know how angry he gets when he is drunk, I shouldn't have pushed his buttons."

"Mom it's his fault," Mark told my guilt stricken mother.

"Shut up, Mark," I screamed. "If you would've followed his directions perhaps he would not have been so upset," cried Mark with revenge in his tone.

After the fall in Pittsfield, no one was the same. Mark and I never played Jai Alai or talked as we used to. Even after our mother's plea to stay happy, the three of us could not feel normal under the same roof. The chief's death left our family without anyone to take care of the farm's only profitable product. For me, his death reflected life's depressing denial of true wealth.

After my father's death I needed a change. Keeping up with work on the farm reminded me too much of my lifeless father at the bottom of the cliff. Now that I was finished with high school, I strongly decided it was time for me to move on. Perhaps, a change from Pittsfield to a location with Jai Alai is what I really needed.

Anna had inherited a minimal amount of life insurance for my father's accidental death. Thus, she supported me, along with my drug addicted brother Mark, for a couple of months. However, the money could only stretch so far and Anna was becoming very tired. Not only was the farm slipping through her fingers but Mark was too. She couldn't bear witnessing another loved one fall victim to substance. As strong of a woman as Mother was, the stress upon her became stronger. It took over her mind and caused her to completely break down. We had no other choice but to sell the farm. I guess it died with the chief.

There was no longer any reason for us to stay in Pittsfield. Anna moved back to Ohio where she spent her childhood. It brought her a sense of security to be "back home." She still spoke with Mark and me, but we rarely ever saw her. It took quite a while for Mark and me to begin talking again. When we left the farm we headed in different directions and simply didn't care to look back. I had decided to follow what motivated me. Jai Alai was beginning to build legendary acclaim in Hartford, which was where my cousin, Jenn, lived. I was confident with my polished ability that I knew I would make a team.

Mark, sadly, was motivated by a different source. He decided to move to Boston some time after me with some of his fellow drug-dealing friends. He used what he received from the inheritance for support. During his childhood, Mark's passion and talent lied in basketball. Unfortunately, he had no other outlet for energy or any reason to attend school once it was repealed his senior year. Strangely, when I told him I was moving to Hartford to follow my dream, he started working out his basketball game every day during the final days in Pittsfield. Before his move to Boston, he read about the first Native American all American basketball player. As Mark watched the Indiana State star play, he became inspired. The similarities in their game were undeniable.

Mark had both an incredible jumper and passing ability. He, in a very nonrealistic way, felt his game paralleled the similarly shaped Indiana State legend. Mark loved Barry Word, and thought that somehow he could be just as good. Up until then, the reality of obtaining a comparable success to Word seemed possible for Mark. Realistically, the closest that Mark ever came to becoming a superstar was keeping Word's 1980 rookie card in his prison cell. For a short period of time Mark became determined to reach stardom. However, after moving to Boston and a second failed attempt with basketball, drug use once again became the only thing that brought Mark confidence in his new environment. Mark had not realized the degree of work necessary to obtain the dream of superstardom.

Herbert always tried to explain to his only two grandsons, Mark and I, that society had created the superhuman superiority of athletes, which made the immediate influencers of life a secondary influence on the majority of society. On one hand, both Adams grandsons ignored Grandpa Herbert's condemning of playing any type of sport. On the other hand, Russell had wanted his boys to bring him reward for their athletic ability, except of course, not if it involved Jai Alai.

In the haunted barn, Russell would relentlessly preach to Mark of his future stardom. This led him to believe that success would come instantly, through the talent of our bloodline. If Barry Word could do it, Mark thought that he could "just do it."

Russell felt that Mark's ability briefly provided the same opportunity for our families overall success as every other American had. However, when Mark was thrown of the team because of individual benefit, it destroyed the slight chance towards wealth Russell had. Yet, I knew it never existed because our father was a drunk. Ignorantly, my father felt it was never available throughout the expansion of a nation. However, my father had over a hundred acres of land to farm on and live off of comfortably. Unfortunately for our family, he had taken everything for granted.

Grandpa Herbert, however, felt all individuals were involved in the partnership of a unified reality. He felt as with sports, only a few gifted individuals have a sense of greatness, and much could be lost by an unfulfilled dream. Grandpa Herbert once told me, "Pat discovering the talent in you that improves all man is where your passion should lie."

Against Grandpa Herbert's advice, I was able to become a successful athlete because of my practice and discipline. In a way I was going to improve humanity by showing off my precise skill. The sport finally helped me find a form of confidence. Jai Alai was my only possibility at success, especially after my gloomy past. I needed to escape any reminder of my father. The passion that derived from his evil became the only thing that I would allow myself to remember him by. With that passion and much practice with my stick, I became very confident in my ability to join the Jai Alai circuit in Hartford. The past criticism by my father only motivated me. After his death, my first move was to earn a tryout somewhere in the professional circuit. A phone call after Russell's fall from a distant relative put me on the correct path. My cousin, Jenn Jartlow, lived in Hartford where Jai Alai had just became established, and she told me that she could easily hook me up with one. She dated someone that was connected to a team roster for the only recently popular foreign sport.

After selling the farm with our mother, Mark and I each took our fifty thousand dollars, and headed towards our destinations of destiny. Mark found a place just outside of Boston with three of his small time business partners. What brought them immediate success in the big city was the sale of Russell's final batch. At that time, Mark loved his new opportunity in Boston, and once the four small town men from Pittsfield established themselves as hustlers, the strongest gang in Boston yearned for their business partnership

I headed south to Hartford a week after Mark's departure to Boston. Fortunately, I had a cousin who lived two miles from Hartford Jai Alai on Broad Street. Jenn Jartlow was related to me through Henri Adams, his brother was a descendant on her family tree. Henri's brother, Matchienthew, before his Americanized name change to Mike Jartlow, also fought in The War of 1812, and Henri told many stories of him in the journal. Both the Jartlow and Adams family remained close through the many generations since Matchienthew's suicide. Jenn, however, was the only living descendent of the Jartlow bloodline. I quickly decided to live with my distant cousin after she offered me free board in the city where my dream lay. Jenn told me she had no problem helping me out while I was in town getting a feel for the Jai Alai circuit.

Jenn Jartlow was able to afford a respectable apartment down the street from where she worked. She was a stripper at a recently established strip club. Jenn's choice of occupation reflected her parent's choices in life. They were Hartford crack heads and she, unfortunately, was stuck in the middle of their dependence. Fortunately for me, Anna knew Jenn's knowledge of deviance and begged her to eliminate any bad from her own life to help me through mine.

The widow knew her son's lifestyle could begin to resemble my father's at anytime. She envisioned a grim picture for her second born, just as it had become for Mark. When Jenn and I began drinking and feeling comfortable, Jenn became the first person that I told about my father's gruesome death. Up until then I had simply told everyone that he died from complications of alcoholism.

Only the Adams family knew how the chief really died. Once his body was dragged back to the farm, and my mother, Mark, and I absorbed his loss, we then buried him behind the cornfield. I was unable to express any emotion until Jenn, on my second night in Hartford, helped me to justify the loss.

We never shared the secret because we did not want to lose the respect of others at the mention of suicide. The questionable fall, which occurred exactly where Russell knew the cliff descended, happened during the most climactic era of my life. I was beginning to establish who I was during the untimely death. Mark already had established who he was, which obviously had not been too effective.

On the second night at Jenn's, after getting home from a stressful shift, she and I polished off two liters of vodka. She then proceeded to tell me, "You have to realize that sadness is contagious. If you decide to keep everything in, you won't be able to recognize the beauty in life and people. As you hide yourself, opportunity will be hidden from you."

Jenn had to strip an average of thirty hours or more a week. It was the only way she could afford both the apartment and an extravagant nightlife. She was not fortunate enough to have any family ties with financial wealth. Her parents had no money for the family. They had selfishly spent their modest income on a hopeless fix. This only made Jenn strive even harder towards any opportunity at wealth.

She had found no other opportunity in Hartford to make successful money after graduating high school than stripping. She made minimum wage at her first job, which, ultimately, made her decide to show off her tight stellar five foot seven body. Her only employment in stripping was at the Silver Club, making triple of what she was making at her first employment.

I felt bad for my hard working cousin, especially, after staying a week in her apartment and eating all of her food. I began working light construction during the end of my first week in Hartford. Following work, I would go to Jai Alai games to understand all the rules. At first it seemed as if only positive things were happening to me after my father's death. I was moving off the farm and exploring new opportunity. Ironically for me, Jenn dated Kenny Carter, whose best friend was the house bookie of the newly popular gaming sport at Hartford Jai Alai.

I did not want to deal with a Jai Alai bookie when Jenn first told me about Kenny's connection. That would initially make my involvement illegal, I would be a criminal, just as Russell had told me I would be. However, not following my father's advice, I insisted to Jenn to set up a meeting for me with Kenny. I did not listen to my father just as I did not listen to my grandfather, Herbert. I should have listened to the only legitimate chief in our family. Herbert was the only Adams to ever make a substantial amount of money, before me. Russell never could legitimately become as successful as his father. Herbert became wealthy with the evolution of tobacco in the country. He understood both supply and demand very well.

Herbert formed a comfortable wealth, selling both brand name, and his own, tobacco, in tax-free Indian reservations. He would sell less expensive cigarettes and his own farm grown tobacco throughout New England and Canada to Native Americans. Consequently, Herbert always profited from the bulk distribution. Many Indians either enjoyed the fresh tobacco, from Pittsfield or a discounted pack of Newport's. Unfortunately, my father could not continue the successful wealth that was left in his hands after my grandfather's death.

With the growth of Herbert's tobacco crop, he made the family farm increasingly profitable. Yet, once he retired and left the farm to his son, all the profit left with him. The chief ruined the farm's tobacco crop with his own hands. He did not agree with governmental control of tobacco, and refused to make a living, just as the government did, assisting suicides. Chief Russell felt as if the government always knew that cigarettes were unhealthy, yet they still chose to profit off of assisting lung damage. It became justice for the profit of cigarettes to benefit the few creators.

Instead, Russell decided to profit off a different substance that caused similar harm, yet had less artificial addictive chemicals. My father gained his only financial wealth through his crop of marijuana, even though my grandfather would never agree with success through illegitimate acts, just as previous rulers had. Russell, however, felt that success had first become available for the many that chose individual justice over universal moral. He assumed justice was presented just to allow freedom for the few who were obligated to a certain virtue. My father assumed the wealthy originally grew strength through immorality. As control was established through the powerful, any act performed to gain control became legitimate. Unfortunately, my depressed father never felt as if he had any opportunity for wealth because of these foul acts.

Before death, Russell would say that control was handed down only to the heirs continuing reign, leaving us Adams with no chance for legitimate success. He went on further to say that wealth became a predetermined fixed privilege. Thus, morals and values correlating with obtaining financial wealth were shaped, prolonging the enlightened and denying the genuine. Chief Russell always told me that foresight is blind to simplicity.

The gap of wealth became obvious to us after Mark's expulsion. Russell shared that he discovered the prolonging of a nation conquered through deceit. He felt some self interested men started America, craving the selfishly stupid to thrive for similarity, which was impossible to achieve. Once I moved to Hartford, I soon began to notice all of my father's assumptions.

Jenn's black boyfriend, Kenny, was a drug dealer who carried a gun. Ironically, he felt that a rising percentage of minorities had begun to obtain worth legitimately. Kenny Carter, however, was an exception and connected many dots for me.

Jenn had met Kenny at the Silver Club, where they worked together. Unlike Jenn, the Silver Club did not pay Kenny. He made his money through clientele. He had many customers that would buy an assortment of drugs that he sold in the bathroom. As the clients called the club and talked with Kenny, they would discuss the pick up that would take place in the last stall of the men's bathroom after payment to the house bookie. Upon arrival, the customer would tell the bouncer Kenny's name and hand him the debt due. The bouncer would then proceed to look at the debt list and then nod to Kenny.

I met Kenneth Carter the first time I went with Jenn to her club, on her night off. She wanted me to meet her boyfriend, because he was very philosophical. The first night we met we instantly became friends. Jenn, being related to the Adams, enjoyed philosophically minded men, which Kenny was like no other. As first glimpse it did not seem that the 6'7" 240 pound man knew anything about the form. He made anyone almost immediately turn around and run after spotting him from a mile away. Yet, once he smiled at me, my worry evaporated. Kenny, like many in Jenn's family, loved his drugs and always enjoyed sharing them with another stimulated mind.

At first Kenny and I began politicking I blew him away with the content in the journal concerning the King Phillip's War and The War of 1812. He listened to every word I spoke on King Phillip's, because he knew nothing of the first civil war in American history. Yet, once I tried to discuss The War of 1812, Kenny interrupted me and began sharing his knowledge on the war Henri wrote so much of. At first he blamed the effect of the enlightened dark ages on society for all recent war. He told me that once the Dark Ages began, truths discovered by the original philosophers on the universe were erased. Thus, the study of philosophy morphed into religious theory.

He then told me that the opinions of my father were hateful in the free land for which we lived. Many great men have come from the same destructive land, yet did not gain acclaim for their morality, because only conquerors had.

The next time we met, I brought the journal and Kenny became very excited. I told him that the journal explained how losing the opportunity for freedom in New England almost happened twice. As in King Phillip's War and almost in The War of 1812, a nation was forced under immoral justice.

Kenny Carter lived in Hartford his entire life and blamed most of the city's corruption on the Hartford convention's defiance to the administration during The War of 1812. The Hartford Convention, as the result of an unconstitutional war, ultimately split the nation, abruptly ending one war and beginning the second American civil war.

Anytime we met, we would always discuss the oppression of our past family members. Kenny told me that I still had to be enlightened on The War of 1812. He thought that Henri and Matchienthew (Mike Jartlow) simply escaped the war, and lived happily in Pittsfield. According to Kenny, the war brought on a separation of governmental control, as taxing inevitably increased in the north the south grew through manufacturing. He was convinced that Hartford had been the landmark of one of the most important delegations for freedom in America during the nineteenth century.

My father would have disagreed with Kenny. The war, in the eyes of American Indians, had no positive. "The British consented to restore the territory as it had been before the war; some attempt was made to the Indians who had been allies of the British, but that point was also abandoned"[vi].

Chapter 3

Native

I became aware through other's experiences that equal justice never existed. My father instilled in me that even though America was named after "a friend of Columbus;" Americus Vesputius,"[vii] John Cabot of England claimed it prior. Cabot claimed the land in "the name of the king of England, in 1497, fourteen months before Columbus discovered the continent"[viii]. His son, who landed "as far south as Cape Cod"[ix], also "planted a banner"[x]. "The Spanish explored mainly the southern portion of North America; the French, the northern; and the English, the middle portion along the coast"[xi]

"The English claimed the northern part of the continent by right of this discovery, yet during the sixteenth century they paid little attention to it"[xii]. However, the English conquest expanded throughout America within the seventeenth century. The profiting Englishmen "had no families, and came out in search of wealth or adventure, expecting, when rich to return to England"[xiii]. Yet, as Russell learned, the English power stayed and was able to conquer America because of the alliance of settlers and Indians, which erected during the 1675 Civil War of King Phillip in New England.

After the teachings of my father, which began when I was six, I always wanted to know more of what Grandpa Herbert had taught his son. Somehow, my father believed he knew more than Grandpa Herbert and only shared his elaborative knowledge with me. Russell told me that the humble word of the Native American was eliminated through the War of Phillip, which was "America's first Civil War"[xiv]. The War of King Phillip was between the English colonists and the Native Americans throughout New England. Grandpa Herbert taught his son all the historical knowledge at home after Russell dropped out of an education of ridicule. Herbert led his son towards the knowledge that equality in America was impossible because of the past immoral acts, which had been ignored for hundreds of years. Russell learned that the first "American Civil War had demonstrated that, for a conflict of such magnitude to be fought, the combatants must have fundamentally different worldviews"[xv]. Ironically, the same immoral conquerors of the New England frontier then became foreign servants due to the influence of material.

The discovery of Herbert's most cherished historical artifact under the remains of one of his family's scattered barns expanded his knowledge of Native Americans and forced him to research all the events that led up to King Phillip's War. He also started researching the other morally wrong war that was described in the historical journal dated from 1810 to 1820. The journal, which was buried under the burnt down barn on the eastern part of the Adams land, described more than just Henri Adam's combat throughout The War of 1812. The context of the journal described wars that Native American's, including a couple of my ancestors, struggled with because alliance was unnecessary for settlers after King Phillip's War.

Henri Adams did all the writing in the historic journal. Yet, there were other relatives whose stories were recorded from previous time periods in the outdated journal. Eluwilussit's story was the first written in the journal by Henri. Henri described his great great grandfather's role before, during, and after the War of King Phillip in Springfield, and then Maine, beginning in 1674. Grandpa Herbert was a legend in New England for resurrecting the history of many depleted New England tribes. He spent his adult life excavating buried facts.

The resurrection of our family's lost story arose when Herbert discovered the journal of our descendant in the foundation of one of his inherited Pittsfield farmhouses. It was this journal that initially led him to discover the true losses of Native Americans. After Herbert browsed the frail journal and the writings mentioned by Henri, from the nineteenth century, he had placed his earliest known descendant in Springfield on a farm. Unfortunately, Eluwilussit's land in Massachusetts was lost after King Phillip's War because he was given cheaper land in the worthless most northeastern part of the Massachusetts territory, which later became Maine. His loss of land, because of the inability to pay tax, reflected both the financial and moral devastation of the original natives.

Prior to finding the journal that described his descendant's participation during the two American wars described, Herbert had learned nothing from his father about the truth of their heritage. Grandpa Herbert researched many New England conflicts after discovering the journal, which at first was for or against the natives, during the initial expansion of the English. These conflicts led many natives, including Henri's descendent; to fight for or against everything they knew and loved. Yet, ultimately they lost what was, and had been for hundreds of years, their home. After sharing the lost stories of the Native Americans within the journal to fellow tribes, Herbert gained a respect throughout New England which made him equal to that of a chief.

Herbert taught Russell that he felt the journal spoke so much of the hopelessness that surrounded any opportunity for Native Americans to rein economically or legally, which they had before the English. This disadvantage formed through unfair opportunity in trade, which empowered the government to the right of land that could not be financially accounted for. Unlike the conquering Spaniards with southern inhabitants, the English did not find the New England native inhabitants "organized into chiefdoms"[xvi]. The Indians of the north were not intertwined in the same "monarchies" as "the southern political culture"[xvii]. During King Phillips War, justice was formed for the economically and legally enriched compliant English adversaries, who, consequently, disabled any chance for a tranquil nation.

Russell felt the journal displayed the many feeble acts committed by the conquering Englishmen. Colonial rule, while manifesting justice, began eliminating the balance of trade amongst colonists and Indians. The Indian's worth in society diminished due to the English interpretation of justice. If not under the same opinion or race of the powerful, inhabitants were unfavorable in nature. Herbert, the original Chief Adams, always reiterated to Russell that the Indians and the immigrating Dutch once lived semi harmoniously in New England, until the English force formed in the destined frontier. "The Dutch were the premier European power in the region in the 1620's, with both ties to both the Pequot's and the Narragansett's"[xviii].

This English force, along with destroying the balance of free trade, justified their theory of God's will by destroying any true chance at equality. God's will was what ultimately allowed Christian settlers to adopt principles of justice to enable their governing nation to set standards for individual prosperity. Native savages, ironically, did not meet these standards.

While in Springfield, Eluwilussit knew the English had formed the "Union of the Colonies of Massachusetts Bay, Plymouth, New Haven and Connecticut, [which] was formed (1643) under the title of the united colonies of New England. This was a famous league in colonial times. The object was a common protection against the Indians, and the encroachments of the Dutch and French settlers"[xix]. In 1674, Eluwilussit knew there was no chance at survival unless he allied with the English, yet he still did not want to betray his Indian brothers

As colonists began eliminating equal rights, immorality became the only opportunity to receive justice from the powerful. I learned from my grandfather's distinctive research that before King Phillip's War, the separation of justice between Indians and colonists began to evaporate as a result of the Pequot War in 1637.

"The colonists had sensed that there must be a state of preparedness, and to that end it was written in the first year's records, June 7th 1636, that every man must have constantly ready for the constables' inspection two pounds of powder and twenty bullets or be fined ten shillings, and there must be monthly training. No firearms should pass to natives under any circumstances. [The Pequot] could only rely on the knife and tomahawk, arrow and ambush."

"The Pequot War, Connecticut's only war, [formed through] the murder of John Oldham and his crew of two Narragansett (July 5, 1636) off Block Island and to the hasty action of Governor Henry Vane of Massachusetts in sending soldiers to avenge on suspects the death of a resident of his colony.

Governor Vane hurried a force of ninety men, to bring back women and children as slaves and to compel the Pequot to give up all who had a part in any of the several murders.

As a result of the massacre in Wethersfield (April 23, 1636), where "they stole upon Wethersfield and killed six men and three women, the colonists [had become aware of] the general preparations Sassacus [the Pequot Sachem] had been making. Yet, if Oldham's murder was a part of Sassacus's campaign there was no evidence of it"[xx].

Consequently throughout many years of this expanding separation, King Phillip became perceived as the king of the uncivilized Indians, only because he was in disagreement with the conversion forced upon the Native Americans. Phillip perceived that many of the settlers were driven by Christianity to justify violence. Wherein fact it became a tool of a foreign power to gain or deny alliance. .

"The Wampanoags had not been Christianized; their Chief Massasoit had shared all he had with the newcomers, but his successors, Alexander and Phillip, found their people pushed to one side and downward and vaunted pledges violated, according to their interpretation, as when Miantonomah of the Narragansetts had been allowed to go to his death at the hands of him they call renegade, Uncas of the Mohegans.

Alexander's sudden (but natural) death they ascribed to poison. Philip, young, lusty, supple, came to the chieftainship, bitter of heart. Thrice was he summoned to Boston for investigation, and returned marveling at the exhibition of firearms he had seen. Ordered to surrender his own till signs of an outbreak should disappear, he remarked that he saw that those he did turn in were distributed among the individual colonists and he reminded the government of the spirit of amity which had been promised to our fathers"[xxi].

Phillip was the son of Massasoit, whose death allowed for the formation of Phillip's rebellion. "During the life of Massasoit, Plymouth enjoyed peace with the Indians, as did Jamestown. [Yet,] After Massasoit's death, his son, Philip, brooded with a jealous eye over the encroachments of the whites"[xxii].

Henri learned Eluwilussit's entire struggle during his hidden childhood in what is now Maine. Henri's grandfather,

Megedagik, who was originally brought to Maine by Eluwilussit after his father died, told a new story of his grandfather's to his two grandsons, Henri and Matchienthew, every night long after the time of Eluwilussit.

Megedagik fortunately kept his grandsons and himself from the war's Eluwilussit advised to avoid. Yet, Matchienthew thought it was necessary to fight for the colonies survival in 1812. He seemed to forget that throughout the beginning of the nineteenth century the three of them were hiding from land prospectors.

Beside Matchienthew's dissension, Henri wrote most of what Megedagik had told him about Eluwilussit's story in the journal. Eluwilussit loved his life in Springfield until conflict arose. "The overbearing of the Springfield Indians, to break their solemn engagement of friendship to the English, as upon pain of death...doth so deify them in their own eyes & deter other Indians (yet our professed & pretended friends) that its high time...to stir up all their strength, to make war their work and trade"[xviii].

After Eluwilussit witnessed that fellow Springfield Indians survived by allying with the colonial force and not the stubborn rebelling Indians in 1675, his alliance with the English became more important than with his fellow native. Eluwilussit witnessed, but never fought in, many unbalanced battles against Indians with the lone intent of termination.

Henri wrote Eluwilussit felt that only the exterminating foreign general's became heroes. The settlers, whom conformed to the justice established by immoral rulers, conquered New England by imprisonment and extermination throughout King Phillip's War. Consequently, the American settlers also became servants to a benefiting foreign power as the Indians had. The New England colonists became governed under the rule of gluttony. My father reiterated that The War of 1812 formed uncontrollable expenditures "[just as it had] before [King

Phillip's] war [;] the majority of an inhabitant's taxes went to the town, after war taxes paid to the colony far exceeded those paid locally"[xxiv].

To Chief Russell, moral justice became extinct once the rule of expansion dominated. However, my grandfather felt differently. Herbert felt that it was hypocritical to let the root of hatred be a predisposition. Herbert told Russell that his evil rivaled that of a slave owner politician whom claimed freedom was equal for all, even though the politician was the greatest beneficiary of the product produced for free.

Grandpa Herbert always brought up Henri's experiences when arguing with his son. However, Russell would come right back at his father and say something like "I felt Henri wrote that in 1812 the same foreign powers, which originally conquered a nation from its natives, manipulated moral theory yet again. Dad, all these acts had to be done to conquer the American frontier." King Phillip's War and The War of 1812 formed loyal colonists who easily were forgiven for their savage acts that supported conquest. Colonialist, during King Phillips in 1675, accepted any destructive act towards Indians that obliged a colonial expansion in premature New England. This prejudice caused the original Civil War of America.

Russell assumed that the conquering rulers expanded the impossibility of equality with the expansion of one assumption. The war against Indians continued through many other wars according to Henri during his role in The War of 1812. Henri could not avoid this war, even though his grandfather had avoided both the French-Indian War and Revolutionary War while hiding in northeast Maine. Russell discovered how unfortunate his relatives were to never steer clear from the violence the North American conquerors had manifested. The State of Massachusetts's militia to fight the invading English during The War of 1812 enlisted Henri and his brother, Matchienthew.

Chief Russell was very informed, all from his father and the journal, when it came to his Native American heritage. Everyone in Pittsfield knew all the unjust events that he claimed supported his culture's extinction. The stories he always repeated about inequality were all read in Henri's journal on King Phillips War and The War of 1812. The majority of the journal's stories were told when Russell was intoxicated, which was at every sporting event of Mark's, selling his agriculture to customers, at the local bar, or pretty much always. All who had lent an ear became inclined to his opinion on the two dysfunctional wars in which his descendants had lost all right.

Russell only quoted the journal when he was drunk, because alcohol made it easier for him to make everyone else aware of the wars that had lessened any chance for their own equality. Luckily for me, Grandpa Herbert did not use alcohol to exploit the past as his son had depended on it to do.

Russell would express to anyone the disenfranchisement he had been predisposed to, even though everyone in Pittsfield knew he was depressed because of all the booze he drank. All Russell wanted was the same peace his ancestors had briefly obtained through hiding in the woods of Maine, avoiding almost all attempts of war to take their land.

Grandpa Herbert wrongfully thought that if he taught his son what he knew of the past misfortunes Russell would hold moral virtues and respect the present. The research Herbert had put in on his ancestor's battles snowballed Russell's thoughts into a disagreement with all authority. Russell learned from this research that the same embargo that the Virginian Republicans greatly favored, prior to The War of 1812, purposely weakened their New England countrymen. These countrymen depended on the halted foreign commerce with the French and English to survive. New England, as a result, was nowhere near prepared financially to support a war, which was declared upon England following the embargo.

It was not until Russell was stumbling drunk that he would explain the big picture of his hatred, which usually only seemed to be fully expressed to me. I was the only one still up on the farm playing Jai Alai against the barn when the chief would come stumbling home from the bar every night at midnight. My mother, Anna, wanted nothing to do with the intoxicated Russell.

One night he shouted out to me while I was practicing the Basque game I loved. He said that once the embargo by Jefferson and Madison was placed on America, commerce and free trade sunk for the many not aligned with Republican virtue. Russell quoted Henri immediately after expressing his political opinion to me, because he had to validate his intoxication. "We were subjected to an administration, which in the year 1806, began a system of commercial restrictions, which they said, would not only prevent effectually, the necessity of war thereafter, but would put us in the quiet enjoyment of the rights and advantages we sought to establish. We have, since that period, witnessed, under the embargo, non-intercourse, and non-importation systems, a continued and rapid decay and destruction of our commerce and prosperity"[xxv].

Every day since I could remember, Russell influenced me negatively. A month before Russell's death, he told me, "By 1812, immoral acts by the dominant had become justified through the expansion of America's justice."

Russell had lived a difficult life and had been ready to leave the unfair world ever since the day he read the journal his father forced him to read. Russell's father, Herbert, felt the journal was a priceless source for true historical accounts of Native Americans in New England. My grandfather felt the knowledge of the past should be obtained to prevent the previous immoral acts from happening again. He didn't want it to spawn hatred, because that is how wars began.

After Herbert found the journal, he researched the validity of his relative's writings on the two wars. Russell was the last allowed to read the journal while Herbert was alive. Herbert had only shared it with his son, which formed Russell's conclusion that unjust acts formed his country's justice. The more he learned about the acts by colonists and then a president, to destroy fellow countrymen purely for an expanding interest, the more he became angered. Russell felt that instead of politicians being the people's servant, they became dictators. All this anger continued to build in Russell for the eighteen-year span after he read the journal and drank everyday. Unfortunately, his anger physically came out either on his sons or wife.

The journal taught Russell that there was no peace in justice, just as the many Indians who abided with the English conquerors discovered. Russell, as his father, had never put much attention on their Native American ancestry until after reading the journal. The writings in it from King Phillips War and The War of 1812 were unknown until Herbert researched all the dates in the journal. After researching the writings by Henri Adams, Herbert discovered that the Native Americans focused on in the journal were all ancestors.

Herbert felt his descendants were fighting in wars inevitably guaranteeing their own tribes genocide. Henri wrote in 1814 that the "administration placed itself by its political movement in manifest contradiction of its own principles"[xxvi]. A war with the sole purpose to conquer land from the Indians was also evident to Eluwilussit during King Phillip's War. Thus, Russell concluded that The War of 1812's purpose was to obtain "Canada and the Indians lands, they want nothing else"[xxvii].

Eluwilussit, the elder known ancestor of mine, had formed a strong relationship in 1670 with an English man living in

Springfield, which ultimately saved him from fighting in New England's first civil war. Henri was Eluwilussit's great great grandson, and wrote his great great grandfather's struggle between right and wrong in the same journal that he kept during The War of 1812. He had heard a different Eluwilussit story every night before bed from his grandfather while he was a child living in Maine. Unfortunately for Henri, the past war stories became a reality when, like Eluwilussit, he was forced into an anti-Indian war.

Henri and his older brother Matchienthew fought in The War of 1812 against the invading English. Henri's most elaborate writings described his unfortunate life as a soldier in the militia. The journal showed my father how immoral justice crippled New England before and during The War of 1812, just as bureaucracy crippled the Indians throughout the development of a nation.

The story of Eluwilussit's attempt at justice, during the destructive expansion reflected in King Phillip's War, proved worthless. Grandpa Herbert shared every event of both wars that were described in the journal to me, but he did not share the context due to the malicious descriptions. After Herbert saw the madness the journal brought into Russell, it was hidden until his death.

Unlike Grandpa Herbert, who shared true knowledge with me, Russell forced only negativity on me. Russell was the one who formed the perception in me that equality never existed in America. Thus, I began to assume, as my father that the destruction of the Native American's equality led to the impossibility of a shared national freedom. My father assumed that once an independent man had become enslaved to a greedy one, the only concern, consequently, became the injustice performed by the savage to justify the enslavement. The hatred towards Native American's eliminated any type of optimism.

Russell told me he lost all hope when he discovered that the destructive expansion had disabled any true opportunity for tranquility. Through Herbert teaching my father all his research, Russell proved that the civil war of Phillip simply continued the wrath of the dark ages.

Russell would repeat these points, along with many others, to me over and over again. Russell, simply, didn't realize his resolve, being that he was always intoxicated. Unfortunately, I took in everything he told me. My father's negativity manipulated my philosophy on life, which, at one time, formed hatred due to acts that were committed hundreds of years ago.

Russell and Herbert's influence on me made me aware that bureaucracy was the only victor in war. I discovered that Henri and Matchienthew (Mike Jartlow) both heard word of severe punishment upon certain Indian tribes allied with the English during The War of 1812. I also learned from my father that the victorious conquer of New England by England after King Phillip's War gave Indians no chance for victory or freedom.

I was not the only one who Russell shared his extremism with. Russell shared his opinions anywhere he went, and always followed it with a quote or fact, just so no one could dispute his opinion. Russell quoted Henri's writings in the journal thousands of times in public. During one of my older brother's high school basketball games, he brought many revelations upon a French man who did not know Canada was once part of New France. The drunken Indian failed in everything but history.

Russell shared with the man a few of Henri's writings from The War of 1812 during Mark's basketball game. He described how Henri felt when he was near Canada with the militia to give the French man an idea of how it was conquered.

"We are involved in a war, the end of which can be no more for seen, than we can calculate the magnitude of the losses which must inevitably be sustained by it. Sixteen months of disaster and disgrace have passed; and we are called upon to rejoice, because our troops have at length crossed our own lines, for the purpose of encountering a 'frightful climate', at the setting in of winter. We are promised that Canada should be subdued in six weeks; and, behold! We have been able to enter it, at the end of sixteen months!"[xxviii].

Russell went on for an hour to the badly informed man about most of what Henri wrote on the war he fought in. "When we come out of this war, if ever shall come out of it, gain what we may by it; even all that is promised by those, who have, hitherto, kept their promises so miserably, let us gain Upper Canada, and lower Canada and capture even Quebec; itself; millions of dollars, at the least; to pay the interest of which, no revenue, even from the most successful commerce; can ever be adequate. Taxation- heavy, intolerable, never-ending taxation must follow these exploits as surely is the shadow does the substance"[xxix].

Herbert did an incomparable amount of research on all the journal entry's historical truths and then taught it to his son, which, ultimately, made Russell very informative. Herbert discovered that during The War of 1812, a deceitful justification by a dishonest administration began the war. Unfortunately, the benefiting majority of the expanding government had "persuaded themselves that they can make evil things appear to be good things, provided they quote Republicans, as the authors of them"[xxx]. Foreign influence on the federal government became more advanced in 1812 than during the extermination by foreign powers through King Phillip's. Jefferson and his secretary of state, Madison, formed the Republican Party that ruined New England trade. As the manufacturers in Virginia collected and then sent out their stock product to exporting countries, many New Englander's did not have any product to supply their own, and, consequently, had no choice but to invest in a more expensive foreign product.

Virginian Republicans ruined any type of beneficial commerce for the majority of New Englanders. The manufacturing politicians of Virginia greatly benefited from the "refused principles of the maritime confederation"[xxxi], as they put an embargo on all foreign trade. Unfortunately, "the evil [that Americans] had suffered so much to prevent was brought upon them. War was declared not withstanding it had been so often and so solemnly promised, that [the] embargo and non-intercourse would keep off war. The cause of our great trouble was, that the French captured our vessels, sailing to the British dominions; and the British captured our vessels, sailing to the French dominions. Before the war was declared against Great Britain, the French [abolishment of] their [order], which before that, had authorized our vessels to be taken; and while we were declaring war here, the British cabinet was repealing and did repeal, their order in council, which had, on their side, ordered the capture of our vessels. About the same time that the news of our war arrived in England, the news of the repeal of the orders in council arrived here"[xxxii]. My father told me all this was created to bring out anger in Americans towards the English, consequently the war was declared months before English cruisers withdrew the order to not capture New England vessels.

Somehow in 1812, Madison declared war upon England because they impressed our sailors after we permitted it. Russell had discovered this once he read the context in the journal that read, there was no "reason why people having no trade, have gone to war for free trade; and why, having no sailors, they continue the war for 'sailors right'"[xxxiii]. Consequently, the compensation from war went directly to the government, not the rightful state of which the forfeiting militia lived. Residence, constitutionally, sacrificed everything for their state's security, defending the invasion set up by the President, yet only bureaucracy was rewarded.

My father took from the journal that "our own government was the most eager and successful, in their efforts to ruin us"[xxxiv]. Madison used "impressments of sailors" as the smokescreen for a declaration of war against England. As the American force expanded north, south, and west to unconquered frontiers before the declaration of war, the maritime English force then invaded helpless America. Both forces had no concern for the French or Indian inhabitants of Canada, who called the unconquered frontier home. The "confederacy of European states"[xxxv] colonization of the Indian's land in America was supported by the many that formed alliance to conquer the entire frontier in accordance with foreign expectations. Thus, opportunity for absolute control of unconquered frontiers belonged to the strongest force.

Russell took all of his father's discoveries in for immense thought. He learned that immoral acts by forcign based government were nothing new to conquered countries. Just as Eluwilussit's story expressed in the journal, "there was no rigid frontier separating the sixty thousand English from the eighteen thousand Indians living in New England on the eve of the 1675 conflict"[xxxvi]. Due to Russell's manifested hatred through reading the journal, my grandfather had decided to share only one written document within it to me before he died and gave it to my mother.

Russell felt, however, it was important for me to be exposed to all the writings through my ancestor's struggles. I became increasingly intrigued by my father's disenfranchisement while he quoted the journal aloud, mainly because of the passion that each word omitted from his mouth.

I was finally able to read the journal after my grandfather died. Herbert gave Anna the journal a week before he died and begged her never to put it in his son's hands again. After my grandfather's death I promised my mother I would not share the journal with anyone who would use it for evil.

Mainly, I could never interrupt my father while he quoted the hand written journal. I listened to everything my father had to say on the expanding conquest through time. Russell perceived it had created many destructive changes amongst civil indigenous cultures. He felt these changes had been manifested by decadence of moral right and ultimately eliminated any common prosperity amongst man.

It was truly deep, but I tried my hardest not to stress about others chaos in the past, just as Herbert had told me. My father, however, disagreed with every act that the English colonists maliciously used to take advantage of Native Americans throughout the construction of New England. However, once my father fell to his death, the strain that carried my burden also fell. After Russell's death, I simply let things fall into place.

Chief Russell proved to be a very humbled intelligent Native American, but only when sober. Under the influence of whiskey, he became the drunken chief known all over New England. He always embarrassed me whenever he spoke in public. Russell, unlike my Grandfather Herbert, was famous only for a negativity, which was narrated to any open ear.

Dozens weekly bombarded by the chief, at the Pittsfield sunset on the cliff overlooking the cemetery, a mile from the Adams farm. After having had his usual influential consumption of Mr. Daniels, he gave the townies some intoxicated knowledgeable entertainment alongside a beautiful sunset. Russell always had to prove how informed on the disadvantages of Native Americans he was. His father's discoveries gave him insight that only came out during his daily binges.

My father's negativity always exploded once he started drinking whiskey. My Grandfather Herbert was also influenced by substance, but it was only nicotine. However, it was responsible for his death. Herbert did not need much to help him share his knowledge in hopes of constructing equality. He did not depress everyone as his son. For Herbert, he knew right, as well as wrong, existed in everything.

According to Herbert's research, the English expansion throughout the seventeenth century ultimately began the end for many of the New England tribes. Chief Herbert had proved this to his son through the devastation of the Pequot tribe during the Pequot War in 1637. Herbert had spent all his free time on researching the relevance of the journal after retiring to the Berkshires, once he gave the farm to Russell. His desire for a historically demonstrative theory was motivation enough. In Herbert's opinion, the English used what they considered to be a series of immoral acts committed by the Pequot's to justify their war, and even though the Pequot War seemed to be a two sided battle, only one side wanted to fight.

Chapter 4
Gift Giving

Grandpa Herbert's research that formed through Henri's writings proved to my father that before the War of King Phillip, the Pequot War was greatly responsible for the permanent separation between the Indians and colonists in New England. Prior to the Pequot War, the security of the English colonists appeared to be in ruins after the death of an English ship Captain. "Hostilities broke out when the Pequot's sought revenge against a Dutchman who, against their wishes, had traded with some of their tributaries. But instead, probably by accident, they killed an English ship Captain, John Oldham"[xxxvii]. The murder of this English captain, Herbert assumed, was the spark that ignited the Pequot war, even though the Pequot tribe, and their sachem Sassacus, had never initially intended upon fighting in a war.

"With false promises and much obeisance to Massachusetts, Sassacus had escaped punishment for that and his awe had not been increased. Now that more white men were coming within his realm and treating him disdainfully, and now that the Narragansetts to the east were in unfriendly mood, and Uncas, his rebellious son-in-law, was courting the favor of the whites, it was time to spread terror"[xxxviii].

According to Grandpa Herbert's historical research, "the English set out with Narragansett and Mohegan allies to subdue the Pequot's (May 1637), who, not coincidentally, occupied some of the most valuable land in New England. The conflict climaxed in May 1637 after the English and their Indian allies surrounded a palisaded Pequot village on the Mystic River". The colonial militia "attacked one morning before dawn, and in the ensuing chaos the village was torched. As for those Pequot men, women, and children who managed to flee the flames, Englishmen, to the horror of their Indian allies, shot them down with their muskets. By the end of the day, six hundred to seven hundred Pequots had died. Most were noncombatants, and most were burned alive"[xxxix].

The powerful English adversaries used propaganda to form negativity towards the Pequots, enabling both Indians and colonist to ally against a common foe. While most Indians were shocked by the war and the brutality by which it had been fought, others were pleased. The Pequots came to dread blunderbusses, short muskets of wide bore and flaring muzzle, formerly used to scatter shots at close range.

Uncas was a native leader in New England and greatly benefited from the outcome of the war. "In the first half of the 1630s, Uncas had tried several times to depose the Pequot leader Sassacus, only to fail repeatedly. When the English arrived looking to avenge John Oldham's death, Uncas found a power that could tilt the political balance in his favor. The aftermath of the Pequot defeat in 1637 saw Uncas' emergence as the grand sachem of the Pequot's and the Mohegan's"[xl].

Uncas took his ex-Pequot admirers and fled from their Pequot tribe to form the Mohegan tribe, which quickly became pro-English. Uncas was "the quintessential example of a New England native who vied for political power and successfully used the assistance of those from another continent to get it"[xli].

The English force, with their Indian allies, had created martial law amongst any Indian not conforming to their English rule. Colonial bureaucracy eliminated moral justice toward Indians. The forming colonies claimed the property of the defeated rebellious Indians only rewarding the Indians whom assisted in the English victories. "Gift giving was so important that colonial governments had to conform to this Indian tradition if they hoped to gain Indian allies"[xlii]. Henri's recordings of Eluwilussit's story, explained how "the Mohegan's, sold plots of ground first to one white man and then to another, often for a drink or a trinket, until there was confusion that occupied the attention of courts in England and in Connecticut for seventy years"[xliii].

Yet, many tribes did not agree with the Mohegan and English partnership. They looked down upon the tribes that converted to Christianity in order to form an alliance with the English. Eventually, the majority of colonists believed it was because of these objections that the rebellion was formed.

At first, many of the older, peaceful, praying Indians refused to join the colonial propaganda. They couldn't bring themselves to kill either rebellious or converted Indian relatives. They were far more intelligent than the English made them out to be, and realized what was happening. Unfortunately, the only chance at survival for Indians was joining the conquering force. Thus, they not only lost their land, but also their freedom. It became a never-ending struggle. Even after fighting and winning battles for the English, the converted Indians were still forced to pay a debt in retribution for their sacrifice.

As the separation of rebelling Indians from converted Indians increased, colonial tranquility with its natives decreased. The English had used religion to justify their savage acts against Indians, for it was God's will to conquer New England. Many Indians who did not join the militia had no other choice but to take what was left of their independence and join the rebellion. Phillip led the Indians, "who opposed the spread of Christianity through Indians"[xliv]."

One quarrel that Eluwilussit disclosed to his grandson, Megedagik, was when "a band of Connecticut men [were led] into Rhode Island, by strategy on April 3 annihilated one band of Indians and soon brought back the Narragansett Chief Canonchet. To the offer of his life if he would secure peace, Canonchet replied that he wished die before his heart was made soft and before he had spoken unworthy of himself. On April 8, the council at Hartford formally acknowledged the receipt of his head from the Mohegans and Pequots to whom had been turned over for execution"[xlv].

The Indians who opposed colonial authority never could be accepted because the English would not accept any disagreement in their beliefs or their deserved retribution. Thus, the Pequot destruction in 1637 polarized attacks upon both the natives and English.

"Massasoit, head chief of the Pokanokets, had made a treaty of alliance with the Plymouth colonists soon after their arrival, and kept it strictly until his death (1660). His two sons were christened at Plymouth as Alexander and Philip. Alexander died (1662) at Plymouth, where he had gone to answer to a charge of plotting with the Narragansett against the whites. Philip, now chief sachem, wrongfully thinking his brother to have been poisoned, was thereafter a bitter enemy of the dominant race. For twelve years there were numerous complaints against him, and he was frequently summoned to Plymouth to make answer. He was smooth spoken and fair of promise, but came to be regarded as an unsatisfactory person with whom to deal. In 1674 it became evident that Philip was planning a general Indian uprising, to drive the English out of the land"[xlvi].

Yet, no war after the Pequot burning was perceived until events in 1675. When "On June 6th, 1675 two Wampanoag

Indians were hung in Plymouth, forcing other Wampanoags to attack English settlers at Swansea in Plymouth, opening the war of King Phillip[xlvii]." According to folklore, "The first blow fell on the people of Swansea, as they were quietly going home from church on Sunday (July 4, 1675). The setters flew to arms, but Philip escaped, and soon excited the savages to fall upon the settlements high up the Connecticut Valley." However, my grandfather told me that through research made by "reliable historians, there is no proof that Phillip possessed any eloquence or was even present in any fight" [xlviii].

Colonial perception of Phillip as the provoker of the civil war was based on his tribal status, which strengthened the negative assumptions upon all Indians. The Indians who had not converted to colonial belief were viewed as deviant. However, those who had were no better off. Colonists began assuming that all Indian were savage. Unfortunately, for the many peaceful tribes, a few tribes only formed the rebellion. The English not only controlled their Indian allies, but also imprisoned the very men winning the war for them.

The War of King Phillip became a civil war once both colonists and their enemies ignited violence through malicious acts. "On November 12, 1675, the commissioners of the United Colonies unanimously agreed to enforce the terms agreed upon with the Narragansetts on October 18 [that ordered the tribe to provide hostages to the English]. "Being people not so acquainted with such ways"[xlix], to this end, the United Colonies raised a one thousand man army under the command of Josiah Winslow to march into Narragansett country and demand that they hand over all Indians who had sought their shelter"[l]. "The Narragansett Indians favored Philip, and seemed on the point of jointing his alliance they had gathered their winter's provisions, and fortified themselves in the midst of an almost inaccessible swamp[li]." On December 18, this the largest army ever assembled in the colonies, after a day of fasting and prayer on the 2ⁿᵈ when the people were told by the government of the Bay Colony that they were suffering judgment for their sins of frivolity, started at daylight for the Narragansett swamp where some 1,200 warriors were fortified with their women and children. And it was Sunday. That such an expedition should be undertaken with untrained men, badly equipped, through snow and into pathless woods, seeming to invite defeat and so contrary to the first principles of campaigning, the fate of the colonies was at stake; this blow alone could give them hope. Homes were few and they and their occupants were being destroyed; approaches were being made even to the environments of the equally unprotected larger settlements; whether this was to be white men's land or Indian's must be decided. Hartford no less than Boston can count this as one of the gravest moments in its history. Guided to the one weak spot in the doubly strengthened palisade, the Massachusetts men led the assault but were stopped with heavy loss. Connecticut, [provided with 150 Mohegan and Pequot], followed to become the easy victims of the warriors who were defending their homes when the wigwams caught fire and the flames, swept by a swift wind, drove all before them down the large enclosure. How many Indians had perished could not be surmised, but it must be that the force had been greatly reduced. "Fifteen hundred of the colonists accordingly attacked them in this stronghold. The Indian wigwams and supplies were burned, and one thousand perished"[lii]. "The Naragansetts had lost at least 97 warriors and between 300 and 1,000 women and children"[liii] in what is now West Kingston, Rhode Island. With the burning of the Narragansett palisade by retaliating colonial force, "groups living within New England became embroiled in the war or at least were forced to choose a side"[liv].

Before the destruction of their culture, settlers depended on the Indians of New England for everything. Both cultures at one time had exchanged fur, food, and money (wampan). Fair gift giving created a strong society between Indians and colonists. "Indians invested heavily in the English political system as a means of preserving their autonomy and, in many cases, a land base"[lv]. Peaceful Indians had no options other than fighting for a rebellion or Christianity, because they were mainly descendants from the larger tribes that once fell to the English. "In 1674 about four thousand successfully undertook the monumental labor of translating the Bible into it for their benefit"[lvi].

Contrary to the peaceful Indians, the rebellious Indians initial approach to war was very effective. The Indian's war methods did not resemble the usual approach used by England in the common European war. The savage Indians used woods as cover, and never revealed themselves during the day. Unlike Europe's practice of one army facing another and fighting until victory, the rebelling Indians would not allow the English to find them. The invisibility of their enemy put the English in a defenseless stance. [lvii]

The early destruction of the war, which the English force withstood during the opening conflicts in King Phillip's War, destroyed the trust of fellow Indians. Even if allied through religion, the Indians were still assumed as savages. With no distinction between the rebellious and peaceful, the Indian and colonial militia began punishing all Indians the same. The colonist's began the cultural destruction due to the unwilling ability to separate Indian ally from rebel. Ironically, it was only because of their Indian allies in warfare that the English conquered. The English had depended on Indians for their own achievement in the new frontier. Consequentially, the Christian Indians, who were allies to the English, were not even viewed as equals. Indians were viewed as "our Indian's by town leaders, which offered a prime example of the way leaders of localities within particular English colonies viewed their relations with Indians"[lviii].

Many tribes who did not want to lose their existence joined the English in hopes of regaining autonomy in New England. Briefly during the beginning of King Phillip's War, the rebellious Indians successfully controlled it. Any chance for victory shrank with the expansion of the English-Indian alliance. Indians did not want to continue fighting for their lost rights any longer. Many tribes became tired of the "cat and mouse warfare"[lix].

Indians that did not join the English committed treason toward their colony and that practice formed the Indian refugee camp on Deer Island. Even though they fought Indians who rebelled, Christian Indians still were enslaved.

Eventually, dependable Indians were "sponsored by officials at the highest level" to be held captive "at Deer Island in Boston Harbor[lx]." The colonists had become forced to perceive that all Indians would revolt. By October (1675), most New England Indians were considered hostile towards the English.

Consequently, the peaceful Indians were stuck in the middle. The colonists felt they committed treason for not joining the militia, and the rebellious Indians felt the praying Indians were committing deceit amongst brethren. The rebellion felt these peaceful Indians did not stand true in the eyes of their rebellious relatives. Eventually most weakened neutral tribes joined the militia in hopes of recovering what had been lost, but colonial rule did not accept the surrendering Indians as proper colonists and the savages became imprisoned based on treason or homeless because of the heavy war debt.

As the diminishing rebellion continued to cause havoc, according to colonists, the strength of Phillip's rebellion began dwindling. The colonists coerced many hopeless Indians into an imprisoned partnership instead of joining the rebelling Phillip. The elder Indians tended to join the English in hopes of preserving their heritage. The younger Indian's fought until death in attempt of preserving their lifestyle.

Phillip was able to combine many shattered tribes within his rebellion, but the majority of Indians did not want to get in the way of bureaucratic rule. The Indians only had two options, fight against the English and kill fellow Indians, or become servants for the English, in which by becoming a servant demanded them to be banished on a frigid island.

"The year before Philip fell, trouble broke out with the Indians to the north, on the Piscataqua. In the summer of 1678 the English of Maine felt themselves compelled to purchase peace, thus establishing a precedent which fortunately has not often been followed in America. The home government was much annoyed at the obstinacy of the colonists in not calling on it for aid in these two Indian wars. Jealous of English interference, they preferred to fight their battles for themselves, and thus to give no excuse to the king for maintaining royal troops in New England"[lxi].

Though fighting continued for hundreds of years after Phillip's War, the rebellious Indians mainly migrated to the unwanted land in Maine of Massachusetts, and also the open Canadian Frontier. In the journal, my descendant, Eluwilussit, was fortunate to avoid any confrontation with or against the rebellion, before and after Phillip's death. Eluwilussit, through the journal, seemed to be an influential Indian throughout the rebellion. According to Henri's words in the journal, Eluwilussit supported the trade between Hartford and Springfield. He had a rare ability to intermesh commerce amongst the colonialists and Indians. Unfortunately for Eluwilussit, it ended after the outbreak of war.

Thus, the war eliminated any opportunity for fair trade amongst Indians with the colonists. The war eliminated any chance at prosperity for Eluwilussit and his family until he turned on his Indian brethren.

Herbert's research showed that a fellow Indian fighting for the English finally killed King Phillip, "August twelfth,"[lxii] ending the civil war in New England. The rebellion, including the deceitful Eluwilussit, surpassed King Phillip's death, traveling to lands less valuable to the English.

Eluwilussit did, consequently, travel to a part of Maine that was away from the rebellion. He wanted to keep his grandson away from any type of violence for his final years of isolation. While hiding in Maine, he advised his grandson to avoid war with the white man at any cost, as he witnessed how the King Phillip's War almost entirely evaporated the original natives of New England. Eluwilussit lost his only son, who rebelled against his father's wishes. He raised his grandson to realize that all the work put in will never amount to respect from some men. Even though many Indians did everything that was asked by the English, they would never have been considered equals.

As time passed and the malicious acts of colonial expansion increased, the colonists continued to not presume any moral theory through government. New England had become foreign-based without any legitimate foundation to build upon. Grandpa Herbert always emphasized to me, because he would not let me read the journal while he was alive, that by conquering America, bureaucracy forgave any immoral act through a God who allowed discrimination. "The eventual victory validated the Puritans' perceived covenantal relationship with God as his chosen people"[lxiii].

When I was eleven I asked my grandfather why King Phillip's War was never discussed in school. Chief Herbert simply told me that "even if, it was the first civil war in America. It had no relevance to a democratic expansion."

My grandfather explained to me that there were not enough Indians in school for the war to be of any significance. Simply, he told me that the horrifying acts of the forming colonists were not chosen to be exposed institutionally.

Chief Herbert, without sharing the actual journal, enlightened me on why the hidden wars have not been mentioned in school. He felt it had been avoided because of the malicious influence that conquering Americans forced upon their own countrymen. The hidden wars, in which my bloodline had fought for justice in, have been prequels to both the Revolutionary and Civil war.

The Indians who continually fought for what they lost, proceeding King Phillip's, had no choice but to welcome French alliance to avoid genocide. However, many Americans could not avoid the increasing debt caused by the Revolutionary and French and Indian War. Eluwilussit, luckily, had taught his lone heir to avoid battle and stay in land unwanted. The few surviving Indians left in New England became Americanized after mating with other nationalities in hopes of salvaging what once was.

Unfortunately for Eluwilussit's only grandson, Megedagik, he was killed because of an insatiable hatred. Both of his grandsons were thrown into a war just as Eluwilussit had told him to avoid. Ironically for Henri, Matchienthew enlisted under his own will to protect the very land his grandfather was killed for. For Matchienthew and Henri there was no avoiding the unconstitutional War of 1812. The brothers, according to the journal, had no choice but to fight for their country in an unnecessary war. I read in Henri's journal that after his grandfather's plea not to enlist, Matchienthew still chose to fight for his country. Once he heard word of an English invasion against his state, he had no other option than to fight. However, after he joined the Massachusetts militia he was sent from Maine out west.

The set up war in 1812 had tormented New England severely, just as Phillip's War did to the Native American culture in New England. My father, Russell, told me that just as King

Phillip's War was against natives, The War of 1812 as well was against native New Englanders.

As the Republican Party formed in Virginia, Jefferson had "remarkable tenderness toward France, because that power controlled Spain, from which Jefferson was eagerly seeking the cession of West Florida"[lxiv]. France's influence on Jefferson allowed America to acquire Louisiana in 1803, even though "complaints were for a long time made to the United States, of the delay which some American citizens had experienced in receiving the [compensation for damage] which were due to them, and of which the reimbursement was made, from a part of the funds destined for the acquisition of Louisiana; but the affairs of the heirs of Beaumarchais, who have in vain, claimed for twenty eight years, a debt made sacred by his motives, proven to the last degree of evidence, and on which the declared interest of the French government does not admit of a payoff"[lxv].

My grandfather disclosed to me that many soldiers who fought in the apparent important battles during The War of 1812, especially the Battle of New Orleans, disagreed with "the necessity under which [the] government found itself of causing its troops to fall back to guard New Orleans against invasion by internal enemies"[lxvi]. With expanded control in the union before The War of 1812, the Republican agenda, thus, conflicted with the ethical federalists in and around New England who had always agreed with constitutional ethic. The acquisition of Louisiana diminished the balance within the government.

The right of militia to be controlled by its own state in 1812 was no exception. Unfortunately, the Federalist Party was quickly losing credibility as their disagreement with the war continued. Grandpa Herbert disclosed to my father that "The vast continent of America [could] not be long subjected to a democracy if consolidated into one government. You might as well attempt to rule hell with prayer"[lxvii].

Due to the influence of relatives, I assumed the opportunity for freedom was only initially made possible for English settlers in America, because the majority of Indians had either been killed or enslaved. After King Phillip's War, Indians no longer tainted the newly established independence for Americans. However, for the colonized settlers of New England, they were still considered natives of England in the conquered Frontier.

After King Phillip's War, the majority of colonists in New England became governed under principles established through a successful revolution. Consequently, with no other option, Indians hid away in Canada with French inhabitants to escape war from the mounting brigade. The destruction against Indian was not complete until North America was conquered. Fortunately for Eluwilussit, he befriended a few Dutch men in Maine, and hid his family in the most Northeastern part.

Henri's writing revealed to my family that up until President Madison declared war against England in 1812, Eluwilussit's descendants were hidden well. Consequently with the exposure of property, my descendants, Henri and Matchienthew, were then forced to fight in the war due to the English impressment of American sailors. Coincidentally, France committed the same impressments, but in accordance with the Treaty of 1778 that America had with France, independence lied upon a foreign country during warfare.

The War of 1812 forced most New Englanders out of their homes to defend the invasion with the state militia. Yet, it was more important for America to have the army conquer the foreign land of Canada, instead of protect the homeland. Unfortunately for New England, the war between the confederation and New England politicians never actually ended until the conclusion of America's second civil war. American seamen impressed on Madison's watch were his only justification for the declaration of war, which tore the nation apart. As Phillip's war settled New England, Madison's war attempted to destroy it.

Russell shared with me, from my grandfather's research, that The War of 1812 had caused a difference of opinion between parties. The few ethical politicians for the people were federalists. Yet, as the con federalists favored a maturing American government benefiting from unconstitutional powers, the majority of the country trusted the war party's likely prosperity. Thus, President Madison's "just" expectations with England prolonged the war, because his ignorance for American's well being destroyed the original ethical party.

The Federalist Party, which contributed to the construction of the Constitution, was losing containment of the manipulating con federalists until Madison's declaration destroyed the party. I knew all this because the destructive expansion in America, which broadened during the war of King Phillip and progressed during The War of 1812, was all recorded in Henri's journal.

The journal excerpts originally shared by my father made me realize that the same wickedness the evolving government forced upon New Englanders during The War of 1812, had also occurred to Eluwilussit during the War of King Phillip. Accumulating after King Phillips, taxation was marked from the war for retributions attributed to their colony. Through Grandpa Herbert's research of The War of 1812, Russell assumed the compensation went directly to the government, even though citizens were protecting their state from the set up invasion by the president.

Unlike Phillip's War, payments no longer went to the state broker during The War of 1812. During King Phillips War, "Broker's"[lxviii] were established in towns to gently explain to town inhabitants the compensation due to the colony for retribution as a result of the victorious war. Inhabitants had no option other than supporting the invincible governing rule.

Local inspired political colonists, whose greatest interest was for the colony had no influence.

As the King Phillip's War concluded, expenditures, debt, and imperial control all increased. Control of New England inhabitants belonged to the crown. Unfortunately, New England colonists did not realize the stability Indians brought to a colonized society. Just as with their loss in commercial trade, "the reduction of Indian political power in New England did not make the orthodoxy of Puritans in Massachusetts more dominant; rather, the postwar Puritans eventually became like a minority ethnic group themselves as the Crown intervened politically"[lxix].

Chapter 5
Folklore

The only reason my descendants had any chance to continue their Indian bloodline was because of an Englishman, who advised Eluwilussit to avoid conflict with the Europeans. Eluwilussit's grandson, Megedagik, only avoided the French Indian and Revolutionary War, while hiding in Maine, because of this advice. Many years after Eluwilussit's death, Megedagik shared Eluwilussit's King Phillip experiences with his two grandsons, Matchienthew (Mike Jartlow) and Henri; which Eluwilussit had told his grandson himself.

Every night under the Maine sky, Megedagik shared a new story about Eluwilussit's role in the war. Megedagik made clear to his grandsons, Henri and Matchienthew, that Eluwilussit's role in his native Nipmuck tribe was very deceitful. He went on to his grandsons that as with many members of his tribe, Eluwilussit had partially joined the rebellion of King Phillip. He was involved in the Springfield Burning of October 8. However, even after Eluwilussit had celebrated with the rebellion, he still continued an alliance with a successful Englishman. Fortunately for Eluwilussit, his existence was not jeopardized, only because of this alliance with the English man, John Pynchon, who taught him not to fight in a white man's war.

Pynchon had greatly depended on him for trade from Springfield to Hartford. Eluwilussit was one of the few Indians who kept his freedom after he joined the Indian rebellion. The English knew the importance of building alliances with Indians was stuck in the middle of the rebellion. "The Massachusetts troops, [were] convinced at last that Indian scouts were an essential, [and] were pressing the devastators hard throughout eastern Massachusetts"[lxx].

As both a practicing Christian and Nipmuck, while living in Springfield during Phillip's War, Eluwilussit was connected to many prestigious directors of war on both sides. Eluwilussit, fortunately, did not become enthralled in the climaxing slave market, which became disgustingly successful due to the experiment with the natives. He avoided war and imprisonment because he greatly assisted John Pynchon with trade to Hartford with the Podunk tribe before and briefly during the war. The inability of colonists to deliver commerce, within the rebellious Indian's jurisdiction, gave Eluwilussit a dangerous opportunity for success.

John Pynchon had led the Massachusetts militia and had been very grateful to Indians whom assisted in spotting the rebellion. Eluwilussit hid out for weeks with other rebelling Nipmuck and Narragansett throughout the Pioneer Valley. He met Phillip a few times. Eluwilussit had a priceless respect for the man who quickly became a king. Yet, Phillip could not produce the money or land for Eluwilussit that it had taken to live and survive in New England. Before Eluwilussit swayed loyalty toward the English, he took part in the "Indian rebel attacks against Springfield in October [that] worsened matters. They not only led to the internment of Christian Indians, but they also triggered a chain reaction that eventually resulted in the United Colonies' invasion of the Narragansett territory. Because the Indians who has assaulted Springfield had for so long expressed their fidelity to the English, their actions left the English bewildered and even more distrustful of Indians professing neutrality. The resulting hysteria among the colonists led to abuses of Christian Indians, which no doubt only aided rebel efforts to get support of the Narragansett. Groups that were not loyal to Philip pointed to atrocities committed by the English against praying Indians to argue that loyalty to the English did not guarantee escaping their wrath"[lxxi]. Fortunately, Pynchon had provided for any need of Eluwilussit in return for all the trade he produced. Eluwilussit also provided all the information he knew...

Pynchon, who had great relations with the natives of Springfield because of trade, always kept many Nipmuck allied with his English interests, even after, some joined the rebellion. According to the journal, one dark night Eluwilussit met with Pynchon and another fellow, Benjamin Church. Church told Eluwilussit that he was sent down by the militia after the Springfield fires on October 5, 1675. According to Church, Pynchon's leniency amongst Indian needed to cease. However, Grandpa Herbert told me that Benjamin Church was truly sent to Springfield because "Pynchon, as commander in chief, planned a campaign which they were unable to execute because of the interference of the commissioners at Boston who demanded annihilation in the open"[lxxii]. Church had no tolerance for Phillip and demanded Eluwilussit to help or become imprisoned for contempt because of his role with the rebellion in the Springfield fires. "Despite having spent the majority of the war fighting for Philip's cause, [Eluwilussit] managed, with some aid from Church, to switch sides without having to face the punishments accorded most rebels who surrendered to English control. This switch highlights the fact that [Eluwilussit] was ambivalent in his commitment to the Indian side and that the Englishman Church recognized it. [Eluwilussit], with his shifting dedication, seemed to be pursuing a strategy of self preservation. When he initially sided with one alliance and then switched to the other, the tide of the war turned"[lxxiii]. Even after Eluwilussit served as a spy for the colonialists for almost the entire war, he never was fully rewarded.

Eluwilussit told the two that the Indians no longer wanted war. "Although the [rebelling] Indians had returned to their homeland and had apparently given up prosecuting the war in other parts of the region, they also displayed a reluctance to surrender; indeed, they put tremendous effort into avoiding detection by the English and Indians hostile to them"[lxxiv].

Church finally confirmed with Eluwilussit that he would commandeer the rebellion peacefully, even though all the captures that Church had made were led by his "company of English and Indian's whom had visions of booty and profits from the sale of captives into slavery, suffering almost no casualty, and killing or capturing hundreds of their enemy"[lxxv]. The militia was unable to detain Phillip throughout the war, until Eluwilussit revealed his knowledge of the rebellions location after Church's peaceful resolution. "Philip was chased from one hiding-place to another"[lxxvi].

Church knew that Eluwilussit was the only one that could approximate a realistic estimation of Phillip's location. Finally, after an hour of threats towards his family, Eluwilussit broke and told Church everything he knew about the rebellion's location. He did not want to tell Church of Phillip's location, because Phillip did not want to fight and had returned home. "His family being captured at last, he fled, broken-hearted, to his old home"[lxxvii]. Later the next day after Eluwilussit's breakdown, a "faithless"[lxxviii] "Indian fighting with Benjamin Church shot and killed Philip near his home on Mount Hope Peninsula on August 12"[lxxix].

Luckily for Eluwilussit's English alliance after Phillip's death, he joined the "British emissaries busy arousing the Indians to war"[lxxx]. After living in Springfield with the deceit that forced King Phillip's death, Eluwilussit took his conscience and minimal commission to the cheapest land in Massachusetts, "Mayne"[lxxxi]. Megedagik left Springfield with his grandfather, Eluwilussit, in 1739 immediately after Eluwilussit's only son's death. Taxes accumulated by the war were so immense that even his English allies could not help the reliable Indian. The "social prejudices brought over from England still survived. Even in New England, official positions were monopolized by a few leading families, and often descended from father to son. The catalogues of Harvard and Yale were long arranged according to the family rank of the students"[lxxxii]. "The theatre of [The War of 1812] was to be much the same as in the French and Indian war. The lines stretched from Nova Scotia to the Great Lakes, but settlement had extended so far westward that Detroit marked the flank of both powers, and Lake Erie was included in the field of operations"[lxxxiii].

During war, the New Englanders increased a war debt, which was made apparent by Grandpa Herbert's research on The French and Indian War. "The colonists spent $16,000,000 and England repaid only $5,000,000"[lxxxiv]. As the younger Indians were fearless for war, the English welcomed the colonist's acceptance of war due to their hatred for all savage. Consequently, the colonist murdered Eluwilussit's only son while he fought with the rebellion in 1738, a year after his only son born. The names of the dead rebellious Indians were never shared in the journal because Henri felt it was unnecessary to write about the destructive side of his family.

Megedagik's father robbed from both Indians and English colonists until losing his life on Talcott Mountain. He, inheritably, could not help from joining the rebellious force hiding along the Pioneer Valley following the war of Phillip. Megedagik was brought to Maine, when he was three, in 1740. Eluwilussit immediately left after the word of his death reached Springfield. He had to protect his lone heir. Eluwilussit continually taught his grandson not to participate in any warfare like his father, which ultimately led to his avoidance of the revolution. Megedagik was mainly taught to not fight in a white man's war unless his land was invaded, because their land in Maine originally belonged to Eluwilussit.

Unlike Megedagik, both his grandsons, Henri and Matchienthew (Mike Jartlow), could not avoid fighting during The War of 1812. The British began invading America, according to Henri, once America declared war. America had as much reason to declare war against the French for impressments as they did with the English. Even though New England already had eliminated most of the native's land and fought in a deadly revolution, America was not yet conquered.

Henri, at nineteen, only wanted to protect his family's land from prospectors with his grandfather and not participate in an unjust war. Megedagik did not want his grandsons to die in battle as his father and son had, who could not succumb to the English theory of civilized life.

Eluwilussit was the eldest and most powerful ancestor of mine who had his folklore shared in the journal. Henri wrote about Eluwilussit's importance as one of the only Indians throughout New England with a politician's power, mainly because of his relationship with both Indian and English.

The few Indians left after King Phillip's War, who had land, were usually only able to keep it if Eluwilussit intervened. His mother and wife were Puritan and taught him very good English. He also understood law very well, which helped many Indians keep some origin of their land for a short time, until courts in England held precedent.

Colonial influence on converted Indians helped the English gain submission of other Indian's land, even with the reward of enslavement. Due to treason and contempt, the theory of savagery linked all Indians to eventually join the rebellion.

Eluwilussit never gained enough support to make a difference in Springfield, because if he helped the wrong Indian he'd become guilty of treason. His life was spent fighting an impossible battle, as he forfeited his land in Springfield as retribution for the bottomless debt he owed the state due to the heavy taxes brought on by King Phillip's War. In return for his Springfield land, he chose the cheaper land in Maine. It was the only validation the colonists gave to his family after his contribution towards "conquering the rebellion."

Following the peaceful death of the eighty year old, Eluwilussit, his grandson, Megedagik, grew strong and wise off the land. He raised his two grandchildren into the nineteenth century just as Eluwilussit would have. Megedagik had preserved the hidden hut Eluwilussit had built as long as possible, until another Indian killed him right outside the manmade hut in 1812. The murderer was informed that Megedagik only had received his Maine property because of his partnership with the evil English, which ironically Megedagik's grandfather had done.

The murderer of Megedagik had heard that he committed the same type of cowardly acts that Eluwilussit had to gain his land in Maine. The truth, however, was that gluttonous settlers originally planted the anger within the murdering Indian. According to the plan, once he killed Megedagik, the prospectors in Maine would claim the block of land where the hut was. The murderer would have received freedom, and some of Eluwilussit's original land in Maine from the statesmen that orchestrated the scheme. The murder went perfectly, except for the fact that Henri saw the entire act a hundred yards away and initially froze during the malicious act.

The disgraceful Indian walked behind the aged Megedagik, slit his throat, and then began to scalp him. The Indian assumed no one saw it and he would not be punished for the murder. With the final sight Henri saw of his grandfather, he had no choice but to avenge his grandfather's murder.

Henri immediately crafted through the woods to interrupt the scalping. He confronted the Indian with a knife to the back of his head and asked why? The murderer muttered to him that Megedagik got what he had deserved, for what he had done to the true Indians. Unfortunately for Henri, after that statement the thirty tomahawk wounds he administered were witnessed. Henri then became an unwilling subject to the state of Massachusetts militia in 1812. To make matters worse, Henri's older brother could not be informed of his grandfather's death. Against his grandfather's advice Matchienthew had voluntarily enlisted as a result of the possible English invasion two months prior to the murder. Matchienthew wanted to fight for America as his father had with the rebellion. Henri, following the murder of his grandfather, did not know if his brother was still alive.

Before his grandfather's death, Matchienthew (later changed to Michael Jartlow) felt obligated to join the "Army of the North"[lxxxv]. Grandpa Herbert told me that before the time of Matchienthew's enlistment, "England and France were engaged in a desperate struggle. England tried to prevent trade with France, and, in turn, Napoleon forbade all commerce with England. As the United States was neutral, we did most of the carrying trade of Europe. Our vessels thus became the prey of both the hostile nations. Besides, England claimed the right of stopping American vessels on the high seas, to search for seamen of English birth, and press them into the British navy. The feeling, already deep, was intensified when the British frigate Leopard fired into the American frigate

Chesapeake, off the coast of Virginia. Jefferson immediately ordered all British vessels of war to quit the waters of the United States. Congress then passed an Embargo Act forbidding American vessels to leave port. This was so injurious to our commerce that it was removed, but all intercourse with England or France was forbidden"[lxxxvi].

Matchienthew was first sent to Boston and then Hartford. His first site of war began during the Battle of Queenstown Heights October 1812 when "the militia, denying the constitutional right of their commander to take them out of the State, refused to embark"[lxxxvii]. After many battles, Matchienthew eventually fled the service in the winter months of 1813 after the Battle of Thames with a fellow American Indian named Gilbert. War was inevitable for my ancestors "during 1812 and 1813, while the Americans were vainly struggling to capture a few petty forts on the Canadian frontier, Napoleon was falling back step by step; and on April 6, 1814, he abdicated his throne, and a general European peace was made. The result was new energy in the American war. Twelve thousand English veteran troops were dispatched to Canada, and expeditions were planned to harass the American coast"[lxxxviii]

Henri, on the other hand, had been forced to join after he avenged his grandfather's murder. Consequently, once Henri became imprisoned, the government claimed Megedagik's land after the death. The revengeful Henri had no choice but to join the militia in 1812 because of imprisonment, unlike his willing enlisted older brother. Unfortunately, both brothers not only had to fight English, but also Indians.

Henri barely obeyed any orders, but because he was an Indian according to his commanding officer, Henri's strategy during battle was hidden survival. Unlike his brother, who took the lives of many during the war, Henri purely took captives. Henri was not pure savage; he had part French in him.

Henri did not have an Indian name because of his French mother who his father met in Maine after his first wife's death. After Megedagik's son's first Indian wife died from an unknown disease, Megedagik's son then met Henri's French mother, whom raised Henri and Matchienthew with Megedagik after their father died while fighting with the rebellion. However, she could not stand the hut, she needed civilization.

Chapter 6

Impressments

Henry Adams, while imprisoned in Maine for his grandfather's murder, was awaiting assignment from the Massachusetts state militia. It is there where he was given a last name after becoming unwillingly enlisted, which had been given by the state. Once again, the war party, during wartime, forced their evil upon the peaceful.

The incredible experiences of his descendents from the first civil war until The War of 1812, were all reflected in Henri's journal. Henri knew that the enlistment was not just, because he was educated from his grandfather, who learned all of Eluwilussit's wisdom. Unfortunately upon Henri's arrest, "the general government had no means of enforcing its construction of the Constitution. It did, however, withdraw garrisons from the New England forts, leaving those States to defend themselves; and refused to send them their quota of the arms which were distributed among the States"[lxxxix]. Henri's knowledge of justice, acquired through Eluwilussit's folklore, could not prevent his imprisonment or enlistment. Eluwilussit lived everyday with the responsibility of Phillip's death, and never wanted a relative to turn his back on another Indian again for justice. That is why, in the journal, Henri focused on the pain The War of 1812 unnecessarily caused on his brother and himself.

Henri wrote that "the militia had belonged to the state; they are the state; for they are the people of the state. They have reserved to themselves, the right of saying whether the cases have, or have not occurred, in which they are to abandon their profitable employments, their domestic comforts, the endearments of home, and the thousand nameless blessing contested with it, for the purpose of becoming sick by living on provisions to which they have not been accustomed; for the purpose of being ordered about like slaves; for the purpose of being exposed to inclemency of the weather, and destroyed by the rigors of a frightful climate, for the purpose, in short, of being made instruments and victims in the sanguinary conflict"[xc].

The declaration of war in 1812, justified by the impressment of American sailors, was placed upon England. The destruction by her maritime power caused the war, even though France committed the same impressments. Consequently, America began the war with only England. Fellow Americans had created the impressments upon themselves within a treaty. France, the other original impresser, rewarded compensation throughout the south and west to certain democratic clubs.

The expanding strategy of Jefferson, and then Madison in the Virginian Colony, began to negatively influence the ethical Federalists in New England. Many Federalists agreed with the English influence after the revolution, for it did not favor the Republicans. Henri continued on in the journal that "The federalists had to continue to act with vigor; for thousands of rich federalists have tasted the sweets of monopoly, desirous of continuing to reap its advantages, will give [non-federalists] votes. This is the frailty of human nature; but as a party, they must act consistently. Let our question be, are you for the poor, peace and commerce; or the rich, war and speculation"[xci].

Fellow conquerors, which had expanded outside New England after King Phillip's War, had constructed a formula to cripple the New England people, and continue the English expansion in America during The War of 1812. The unnecessary war with England became forced upon New England by both enemy and countryman, which had trapped New England's security and commerce.

England had no intention of declaring war on her fragile daughter. Yet, America still went ahead and declared a war based on their alliance with France. The most unfortunate thing then happened to America. The French dominance ended in Moscow and the two world powers became balanced. The elimination of America's dependence on the French, "by which the Americans bound themselves to guarantee the colonial possessions of France in case of a defensive war[xcii]," destroyed their front against the English.

Once France retreated to their deaths in Lithuania, America became in the sole control of the English. The English fully amused the commerce of her daughter. As tax accumulated for war by the inflating government, freedom and independence decreased. The English power that had been controlling the seas eliminated all beneficial trade for New England. Money and authority during The War of 1812 began a national separation.

The English, based on their rule over American Englishmen, were able to claim their seamen from the American frontier. "As England, fighting Napoleon single handed and distressed by desertions from her navy, thought to search American ships for seamen and then to impress English tongued men who really were from America"[xciii].

Yet, "There were signs that England would quit her folly while Napoleon's France would not, when news came that war had been declared against England, the very day after England had repealed her orders"[xciv]. The declaration of war had came from the cabinet of Madison, who did not have concern about making soldiers slaves, just as my relatives Mike Jartlow and Henri Adams became.

Matchienthew ended up similar as his brother, with a new name, Mike Jartlow. When Mike left Hartford, his first battle was with "General Van Rensselaer, [who found] his men were eager for a fight, sent a small body across the Niagara River to attack the British at Queenstown Heights."[xcv] After the battle they headed south because the militia refused to conquer the Canadian frontier. They knew it was unconstitutional.

Grandpa Herbert's discovery of Henri's journal taught him through his descendant's struggles that there was no equality in war due to the expanding dominance. It had become strengthened by the greed for an extra penny. The accumulation of past foreign debts seized individual freedom, all for party benefit. Unfortunately for me, Grandpa Herbert only shared the entirety of what he had learned through the journal and his research to my father.

After Russell finished reading the journal during his home schooling, he manifested all the disadvantages Native Americans had since their civil war. He assumed it was impossible to break free of the disenfranchisement of his heritage. After reading the writings of his descendants, Russell knew that all the roots on his father's side had invested all their spirit in attempting to break free, yet never could truly become free after fighting for it.

Wealth or success became impossible according to Russell Adams. My father's negativity did not have any influence on his wife's perspective, though. Anna Adams felt that good had become forgotten through time, just as her husband had always gone out of his way to notice only wrong. She did, however, agree with Russell that past bureaucracies ruined many peaceful lives and manifested devotion towards money. The invincibility, created without any consequence, wrongly influenced a society to believe it was invincible.

Chief Russell's American Indian heritage, and Anna's Basque heritage, left their two sons at the end of the technological spectrum. My parents created their inevitable balance in Pittsfield farming corn and other agricultural tasks. Russell inherited the farm after his father's retirement in the 1970's, which had originally been built by Henri Adams and Gilbert Gardenier after they escaped fighting in The War of 1812.

Henri was going to be sent into Canada, just as his brother had been sent during his enlistment. He had been first sent to Dayton from Maine, and then later to Detroit to join the army of the west, which was returning from a failed attempt to invade Canada. When the army reached Detroit, their main objective was to protect an unarmed vessel traveling to Detroit. It was to drop off wounded soldiers and confidential paperwork, which was absolutely not to get in England's possession. Unfortunately, Henri, and the militia, had no other option than to surrender accordingly with their brigadier's request, General William Hull. The army was not informed that the ship was carrying a trunk with official correspondence of numbers and location of the army of the west. "Hull was brought to a disgraceful capitulation on August 15, 1812"[xcvi].

Unfortunately for Hull, according to Henri's journal entry from August 1812, he did not have enough guns or food to compensate his own men, sparing them from any significant battles. "William Hull at Fort Detroit; was the first victim of such frightful inefficiency as that of Dearborn, in command of the Army of the North"[xcvii]. These inefficient military acts were mainly the result of Madison, who "like most statesmen of his day, had been deceived by Napoleon, as Madison's administration had destroyed such signs of national defense as had been left"[xcviii].

As Henri and the western army retreated "amid the tears of his men, it is said, and without even stipulating for the honors of war, [Hull] surrendered not only Detroit, with its garrison and stores, but the whole of Michigan"[xcix].

Before General Hull retreated due to a depleted army in Detroit, he "prepare[d] to attack Fort Malden, he learned that the enemy were gathering in force, and had already captured Fort Mackinaw"[c]. "In Canada, his men had been summonsed to assist Colonel Lewis Cass and Lieutenant Colonel James Miller. After having seized a bridge over the River Aux Canard, Henri, and Hull's other men, were to control the bridge, then invade the English Barracks, Malden, also known as Sandwich[ci].

"General Hull performed the questionable conduct once he omitted to advance to the bridge seized by the American force. Consequently, the Americans could not maintain the bridge or penetrate the English barracks and retreated. General Hull allowed the English to collect and combine their force against the force on the bridge. He, therefore, retreated with his men to Detroit.

"The expedition of large bodies of men across the river from Detroit showed that the experiences of the revolution threw little on the matter of necessary stores across such stretches of wild country"[cii].

The journal, according to my father's assumptions, disclosed that almost all the land conquered during The War of 1812 in Canada ultimately became an English conquered frontier. The President felt that America should sacrifice its own troops to an overwhelming foe, who reined Canada after America battled the French and Indian inhabitants.

As the western army had retreated throughout Detroit, Henri departed southeast with an Indian named Gilbert, who he had befriended in Detroit while serving under General Hull. The two had quickly become friends as they discovered each other's Native American Heritage through late night talks, which began once Gilbert joined the western army in Detroit with Henri's Massachusetts platoon. He told Henri that his father was French and mother Native American and they acquired land after the French Indian War in Massachusetts.

The two cried for many hours, discussing the deaths of all the rebellious Indians killed by the same army of which they belonged to, as well as fellow friends killed by the English. For Henri, the inability to stop his grandfather's death was discussed more than the unnecessary war, which Gilbert always complained about. Strangely, he told Henri that he would re enlist, even though he felt the war had been created by Madison to enslave the union, and destroy peace. On the journey to Pittsfield, Gilbert told Henri, "the Americans were assisting the cause of a great tyranny and a great commercial monopoly"[ciii]. However, Gilbert's main intension was to guarantee freedom for the future.

The two had both lost at least twenty pounds since their enlistment. Henri no longer wanted any role with war. Gilbert, however, only needed a break. Gilbert told Henri his plan to flee the disorganization in Detroit to Pittsfield, which would house the two if they fled.

After Hull's folly in Detroit, Gilbert and Henri both agreed to leave one night to Pittsfield from their depleted platoon, after spending weeks in the woods of Lower Michigan. All Gilbert wanted was to be with his family, who still owned and maintained the farmland during his departure. Henri never wanted to look back to his revenge and all the soldiers who were dropping like flies.

Gilbert told Henri, that they had nothing to worry about and it was necessary for the two to escape the malnourishment of war. Gilbert knew that the army would not notice that the two had left. They were expendable, even though the two had displayed superior ability in many skirmishes. They knew the army would never have any desire to promote.

Once freed and alone, the two continued to reflect on their time in Detroit. Yet, Henri mostly continued to share the many nightmares of his grandfather's murder because he never could return home. All the feelings of guilt made him want to tell his brother, Mike Jartlow, who may had already been killed in battle. Gilbert heard many great stories of Henri's grandfather, before Henri got going about the attempted scalping and murder, of which his brother had no idea. Finally at dusk the two vanished east for good without any significant worry, because the records were barely recorded.

As the two spent a month traveling east through the Vermont woods at night avoiding any inhabitants, they finally reached Pittsfield. Luckily, the two brothers had acquired immaculate craftsmanship and survival skill through the war. Upon arrival in Pittsfield, they began scouting land on a hill a few miles from the Appalachian Trail on Gilbert's family's land that he loved. They built their farm in only three months.

Within a year of living on the farm, Henri and Gilbert had made just enough money from their agriculture to maintain the entire tax on Gilbert's land. Once their farm was recognizable, the two had again become recruited for enlistment. Gilbert and Henri, once again in 1813, were recruited for the same war they had already fought in. However, with the existing rule and two brother's living on the same land, only the eldest had to volunteer and the youngest was spared. Henri avoided the war because Gilbert told the recruiter that Henri was his lone younger sibling and luckily was able to stay on the land they paid taxes for. Gilbert did not mind the second recruitment, as he was always yearning for the same "freedom" his father had.

Consequently, Gilbert joined with "Backus, his dismounted dragoons, and other detachments, [forming] three regiments

[in] Pittsfield"[civ] and then marched to Hartford. Before Gilbert's departure, Henri promised his Indian brother that he would work with the sun to strengthen the farm unto his return from duty, because he knew Gilbert had already survived war once. Gilbert and the gathered Hartford militia marched away from Hartford towards Canada.

As the force marched, Gilbert felt as if he met a familiar spirit, which he shared with Henri, according to a journal entry. Another Indian from Hartford had discussed many battles against other Indians late at night, just as Gilbert had with his Indian brothers during his time under General Hull. Gilbert again joined a pact of midnight Indians and discovered Mike Jartlow's origin.

After connecting the dots, Gilbert and Mike discussed Henri, the farm, and all the unnecessary deaths during the last two years of the war, except Mike's grandfather. Fortunately for the two, when their regiment had become led by General Harrison, they "[mounted] at Malden, which [they] found deserted, Harrison hotly pursued the flying enemy and overtook them on The River Thames. Having drawn up his troops, he ordered Colonel Johnson, with his Kentucky horsemen, to charge the English in front. Dashing through the forest, they broke the enemy's line, and forming in their rear, prepared to pour in a deadly fire. The British surrendered. Johnson then pushed forward to attack the Indians. In the heat of the action, a bullet, fired by Johnson himself, struck Tecumseh. With his death, the savages lost all hope, and fled in confusion"[cv].

After winning the battle in 1813 which "virtually decided the war"[cvi] and the discovery of his brother's location, Mike no longer had any desire to kill. Mike did not return back to his home in Hartford. Instead he snuck away with Gilbert two nights after the victory. Gilbert had once again escaped from the war with a descendent of Eluwilussit.

Another major factor for the pair's departure was not receiving sufficient compensation from the government for their sacrifices. All the negative factors of war made Gilbert very happy to once again be headed back to Pittsfield with another Indian brother during enlistment. They obtained horses from fellow Native Americans of the Oneida tribe in northern New York, after walking their first week through western New York.

The Oneida were similar to Mike and Gilbert; They were not pleased with their reward for their effort in victory. The Oneida's told the runaways that the authorities lied to them. The tribe felt they did not receive the money promised to them for allowing the seizure of their arms and horses. The militia was no longer rewarded as the original intentions had presented.

When Gilbert and Mike finally reached the farm in Pittsfield on horseback, a beautiful twenty-year-old Indian surprisingly welcomed them. Julia became Henri's wife while Gilbert met up with Matchienthew during battle. After the spontaneous introduction, she welcomed the two with a kiss and told them that their brother had been in the barn waiting a lifetime to see Mike, and ten months to see Gilbert. She gleamed as Mike sprinted towards his younger brother.

The two real brothers enjoyed each others company for several hours and Henri took everything in, which he later wrote about in the journal. The three discussed many of the events they had endured during the war. Tears were dropped once mention of Mike's grandfather came up. Mike was hoping to spend a little time with him in Maine with his brother after their reunion in Pittsfield. Unfortunately for Mike, Henri told him the entire story, which left no conversation for the duration of the day.

Mike was sick of death and working for no return. He decided to stay on the farm for a year with his two Indian brothers who built it. He had changed entirely from how Henri knew his brother in Maine before the war. Mike had flashbacks every night after his tour's of duty. All the dreams were about killing other Indians who allied with the English or French.

Mike could not be around the always happy Henri and his recently pregnant wife any longer in 1815. He found no joy in life. Mike decided to head back to Hartford, which since his departure had evolved industrially. Mainly, Mike wanted to start a family similar to his very lucky brother. Gilbert also left the farm that he had built with Henri to go back to the Gardenier family farm, which had become neglected after his father's death and his reenlistment.

While arriving back in Hartford, Mike quickly got carpentry work and used the farm earnings saved and given by Henri towards land just below Windsor. He built his own house and many others, living comfortably with his wife and three sons in Hartford until his reoccurring flashbacks of war could not be contained. He quickly became homeless after his estranged wife sold the house and moved the boys south to Wethersfield. No one could handle his nightly fits.

Three months later Mike killed himself leaving a note, which explained how he was unable to control the memories of his own savagery. The suicide note was the only excerpt from the journal that Grandpa Herbert had shared with me before his death. My grandfather did not want the journal to create any more hatred in his family, but wanted to show his grandson the trouble that war brought. Henri was able to get the note left on Mike's body, from his widow in Hartford, which reflected his pain from the flashbacks of war:

> "Alas! If all human charity be not dead, in the
> hearts of men; if all tenderness for our fellow
> beings, for our countrymen in arms, be not
> frozen in the once generous bosoms of

Americans, if judgment be not fled to brutish breasts; if men have kept their reason, who shall picture to himself the poor soldier, smarting under the torture of his frozen limbs, burning with fever; writhing under rheumatic torments; with wounds, deep and dangerous, wounds that have not yet ceased to bleed; who shall behold him, even in fancy, creeping from his hard and desolate bed of straw, wrapping his scanty blanket around his feeble, his diseased, his shivering body, and huddled, packed close, with many others, more tortured perhaps than himself, in an open sleigh, exposed to the inclemency's of a frightful climate who shall behold this scene without horror! Who shall be able to contain the wrath that swells his honest, his patriotic heart? Follow, I beseech you, though it be but with the mind's eye, follow the unhappy victim of governmental insanity, but a few miles on his fatal journey; behold the pale influence of death on his hollow cheek; behold his sunken eyes, retiring from the light of the sun; listen to the piteous moans, to the convulsive groans that issue, in hollow and awful agony from his dying body; and if perchance, and before his tongue has forgotten its office, you hear him sending up his curses to the throne of judgment, partake not, I conjure you, in their guilt who have forced these curses out; partake not in it, by defending, by supporting them. Think not of glutting their insatiable fury, by offering up a new and greater sacrifice of blood to their ambition and ignorance! The curse of God is upon them; shun, avoid them as you would pestilence; as you would your souls' eternal misery"[cvii].

My Grandfather Herbert's knowledge obtained from Henri's writings showed that our relatives had no possibility for a free reality. Herbert told my mother that the journal had to be passed down, but not until I was older. The journal my grandfather had found building the new barn, was given to my mother just before his death. It was not to be given to me until I was mature enough to use it for good. Herbert knew that Russell would either burn it or use it for wrong. Anna gave it to me after Russell's death, because she knew I did not want to become as my father.

I, luckily, did not become negatively affected by it as my father. I was able to create my peaceful balance as Grandpa Herbert had, especially after my father's fatal fall onto the Pittsfield cemetery. The balance of knowledge from the journal was the only prevention from giving up Jai Alai after the fall. Realizing that the past presented the future, after my father's apparent suicide, fueled my dream. Russell had endured self denial because of his battle with the bottle, it was in our bloodline.

Honestly, at one time I did feel the strain my father had due to his disposition. Only through reading the journal my grandfather cherished, and Russell's untimely death, did the strain begin to dissolve. I had learned through experience that worth could only be measured by the love I have for myself, because if I did not have that I could not love others. It was the opposite of my father's philosophy, which had no concern for self, just as our descendant Mike Jartlow had not.

Change of opinion occurred numerously, but I never chose the truth until Russell's fall in Pittsfield. Ultimately, it changed all of my negative assumptions. My virtue finally rested on revealing the same hidden truth of life as my deceased grandfather had spent his entire life discovering. I intermeshed all philosophies, because I could only understand my family's virtue. I gained spiritually from my mother, discipline from my grandfathers, negativity from my father, and wisdom from Henri's journal. I formed moral virtues, instead of the virtues held by expansionists, which was formed upon a destructive gluttony.

My mother's side influenced my spirituality, mainly because Jacques felt the only way for unity would be achieved by sharing the past to understand the future. Jacques had a similar origin as Herbert. As with Russell, Anna's ancestry dated back to the settlers of Maine, intermeshing Natives, Canadians and Americans. My mother's side consisted of the pairing cultures, which then migrated to Youngstown, Ohio. The move was forced after displeasure with the invasion of their home state, Maine. The destructive invasion brought the family disapproval towards the Federalists of Maine after they opposed the certain war of 1812, which had no force to withstand the English invasion. Herbert disclosed to Jacques Matchienthew's initial fear of invasion, "Napoleon was falling back step by step. The British now attempted to invade the United States; the Maine coast was occupied, almost without resistance, as far south as the Penobscot"[cviii].

There were many discussions between my grandfathers on why Jacques descendants migrated west. Herbert revealed to Jacques that Maine did not separate from the state of Massachusetts until 1820 and "in 1811 even Massachusetts had chosen a Republican Senator"[cix]. He also shared with Jacques all of Henri's writings and compared them to his descendant's inherited opinion. He brought Henri's journal with him to every family gathering with Anna's father.

Henri wrote on that "when we first drew the sword in this war, I was aware that much distress and many privations must be endured; but I did expect, that all classes, particularly the war party, would join like a band of brothers, in alleviating the calamities incident to a state of war. But how great has been my disappointment, on perceiving that the rich of both parties are only intent on oppressing the poorer classes. The spirit of monopoly seizes with avidity on the most trivial articles, provided they be of indispensable necessity to the poor man"[cx].

Anger from Anna's family began during The War of 1812 while they lived in Maine, according to my Grandfather Jacque's rendition of our family's narration. As a result, the English invasion upon the inhabitants of Maine made "the complaints of the suffering poor become the symptoms of disaffection"[cxi]. Thus, New England's American jurisdiction had become in jeopardy to relinquish the once founding province. Herbert and Jacques enlightened each other every time the two talked.

Herbert told Jacques that Maine was easily invaded because there was no army, and as a result New England had no choice but to summon the inhabitants of each defenseless individual state. Consequently, the army was off conquering frontiers out west and in Canada. Jacques, through Herbert's knowledge and the stories in the journal, finally learned the true maliciousness by the administration in 1812.

Herbert shared with Anna's father that Eluwilussit, unfortunately, was one of the first to learn America's original principles were immoral. The invincible power disabled any chance for equality amongst Indian. Ultimately, the dominating power of 1812 "allured but the more surely to destroy"[cxii]. In 1812, bureaucracy had control over individuals accordingly with the Constitution. It denied each individual state control of their own militia, because an invasion was forced upon the Union.

The only possibility for peace, according to Herbert and Jacques, was sharing universal truths. They both felt that world peace was destroyed once expansion grew through violence. Herbert also learned a lot through Anna's father, who was a well traveled French gypsy. However, Herbert's knowledge was far greater than Jacques.

Herbert told Jacques that his descendants were not right for blaming the Federalists for the problems due to the War of 1812. Herbert told him that the Adams family was so fortunate to have kept their property in Pittsfield during the war only because of ethical federalists. He told Jacques that his descendants were wrong for being upset with Federalists in Maine. The Federalists were formed to only appear as evil. Unfortunately, the Federalist Party was ruined by words and other's immoral actions, because they did not agree with the unconstitutional declaration of war. Herbert felt his relatives had believed the "popular garb"[cxiii] used by the certain men in the government to demonstrate the accordance of war, even though "seamen's rights and commercial privileges were but pretences to prosecute conquest"[cxiv].

Herbert went on to Jacques about how Maine had no choice but to enter the war because the Massachusetts politicians determined their fate. They were being invaded because of their own president's declaration of war without a defending army. The declaration of war forced the inhabitants to become under the control of the government, not the state being invaded by the English force.

Anna had been taught the same perspective as Jacques'. Their descendants had survived the invasion of 1812 and that is all she knew. She was happy to learn the real truth from Herbert. However, she was still very concerned for her sons' survival in the ever changing society. Worry, especially, came after thinking of the past acts of the Adams and Jartlows because of their mental history. She told her sons after Russell's death that "along with remaining true to the family's ability to survive, use the energy passed down toward sculpting your survival. Indians did not have need for religion or war before their land was invaded, because everything in life depended on the same sun, as your grandfather Herbert had discovered."

Yet, I had difficulty sculpting my importance during childhood. Chief Russell permanently instilled his negativity of life in me, which had been manifested by a depressant. The chief was always drunk and depressed about his predisposition that the invincible power put him in. Unlike my father or brother, I had full control of my rationalization of reality. I was the first Adams to graduate high school.

Chapter 7
Kenneth Carter

After high school I received no education. However, there was a different form of knowledge, in Hartford, after I met Kenny Carter. He was more than just a drug dealer and my cousin's boyfriend. To begin, he had a much broader philosophy than mine. According to Kenny, it seemed that Americans became frightened to discuss the reality of past acts. I was different than his assumption of Americans, because he was not familiar with the Native American culture. He quickly discovered that my philosophy was formed through the negative perceptions of Chief Herbert's knowledge. Kenny, after reading the journal within a day of his second encounter with it, quickly understood the strife that my father had formed. He would have read the entire journal the first night we met in the strip club if we had not talked for four hours about Kenny's knowledge.

Like me, Kenny was a minority, yet a white family took in the black youth after his parents had died in a fire. After the death of his parents, he became academically aware while living with a Polish family and attending high school.

This lifestyle change, however unfortunate it had initially seemed, proved to be rather beneficial for Kenny. It provided him with all the means necessary to develop a potential that ultimately landed him in college where he excelled not only in the classroom, but also on the court.

Kenny received a basketball scholarship, and almost had a stellar academic and athletic career at the University of West Hartford. He was so good that the Knicks in the second round with the forty fifth pick drafted Kenny Carter in 1978. He, also, earned a political science degree, which he used to enlighten me.

Unfortunately, drugs and a gambling debt put an end to his superstar lifestyle. Somehow he still was able to keep his spirits high. Simply, Kenny was grateful to be alive and free. He made me realize that the most just of men, who practiced the harmony of ethic, had been silenced from American society due to hate. Unfortunately, the opportunity for a harmonized nation dissolved as man permitted the legal claim of fellow man without any punishment.

Kenny then told me that he researched enormous amounts of text on slavery, yet none on Native Americans. He disclosed his disgust by saying, "In 1619, the captain of a Dutch trading vessel sold to the colonists twenty Negroes"[cxv].

He was disgusted with how slavery continued even after the Constitution was established. He learned that slavery mainly continued because of acts like the one in Kansas when "an overwhelming force of armed invaders from Missouri, whose fraud and violence produced a pro-slavery government. The rigged elections had given Kansas a Slave Code that punishes anti-slavery speech with death"[cxvi].

Kenny continued on "Judge Samuel Sewall issued the first public denunciation of slavery in Massachusetts, in a pamphlet issued in 1700, wherein he denounced "the wicked practice." But the colonists in general saw nothing in the system to shock their moral sense, and it was not until the Revolution that anti slavery ideas began, in New England, to spread beyond a narrow circle of humanitarians"[cxvii].

He believed that "slavery [was] so frightful an aspect to man accustomed to Freedom, that it must steal in upon them by degrees, and must disguise itself in a thousand shapes, in order to be received"[cxviii].

Kenny lectured that his roots had also withstood formidable elements in the American frontier, just as mine had. Kenny's father, a fifth generation descendant of Nat Carter, was to first share Nat Carter's story to five year old Kenny. It began as Nat initiated an escape from Virginia, and headed north in 1810. His journey eventually led him to Hartford, Connecticut, where he stayed and worked. Kenny shared a new story of Nat's life with me at almost every encounter.

He would explain how Nat's success in Connecticut reflected the intentions that were proved through slavery. According to Madison's Inauguration speech, Nat only became a paid employee because of his "conversion from aboriginal neighbor from the degradation and wretchedness of savage life to a participation of the improvements of which the human mind and manners are susceptible in a civilized state"[cxix]. The validity of Madison's words, along with the values of the man who had been elected president, reflected the inequalities formed against Americans by fellow Americans. Kenny, as often as possible, would teach me the manipulated theory of justice at the time of immorality.

As Kenny's story had it, while Nat was in Hartford he witnessed the same suspect administration that was recorded by Henri in his journal during The War of 1812. Kenny described to me how both countryman and enemy were cornering New England. Even though I had already told him I knew of this deception through the journal, Kenny continued. Once Kenny began his inflated knowledge I could not get a word in. He told me that the war caused great worry to New Englanders who were aware of political obligations.

To think impressments were a problem as a result of The Revolutionary War was the greatest American folly. The ability to "impress on the pretext that they were English born" was familiar to the United States long before The War of 1812. "France and England [previously] sought to limit American commerce by capturing vessels for violations of international law." According to law, the Rule of 1756 established "that were a European country forbade trade with its colonies in time of peace; it should not open it to neutrals in time of war." The problem arose when "the United States denied Great Britain the right to interfere in their trade with the French and Spanish colonies."

When the "French ordered the capture of vessels loaded with provisions on May 9th, 1793 and later the English on June 8th, the Rule of 1756 again applied." The treaty of 1778 "expressly excepted"cxx the French order. Even though both countries impressed our men, the British had superiority on the ocean.

I had to realize that the words of Kenny were based on Nat and, also his education. His educational advantage, combined with his knowledge of his descendant's experiences, formed his philosophy. Everything he told me had some significance in shaping the world of today, and his eagerness to do so made his stories sometimes hard to follow.

According to Nat's story, the Union excluding the ethical Federalists in New England had begun the war in accordance with the French disposition. Unfortunately for the Federalists of New England, the only party benefiting from foreign power was the Virginian Republicans.

"In 1811 the Continental System had broken down because Russia would no longer cut off the trade in American ships. The result of this breach was Napoleon's Russian campaign of 1812;

his success would have totally excluded American commerce from the Baltic and would probably have resulted in the overthrow of England"[cxxi].

Yet, with Napoleon's flee of Moscow in 1812, the American chance against the English was buried, along with the helpless French army in Lithuania. The decline of French dominance allowed England to regain total supremacy over America.

Kenny told me "enough has been quoted to show that Mr. Jefferson was not friendly to the Constitution; and some of its friends in the soundness of his general political principles."

"Of this description were his remarks on the Massachusetts insurrection. So far from considering rebellion against government an evil, he viewed it as a benefit, or as a necessary ingredient in the Republican character. He thought it highly useful in its tendency to warn rulers, and that from time to time the people possessed the spirit of resistance."

"Particularly would the public feelings be shocked at the cold blooded indifference with which he inquires, what signify a few lives lost in a century or two? The tree of liberty must be refreshed from time to time with the blood of patriots and tyrants. It is its natural manure."

"This language would better become a Turkish Sultan, or the chief of a Tartar horde, than a distinguished Republican, who had been born and educated in a Christian country, and enjoyed all the advantages to be derived from civilization, literature, and science"[cxxii].

Supremacy grew through the control wars brought because it formed the calculated expense (debt). For assisting the supremacy, architects of war were rewarded with both power and money. A passive administration expressly excepted English and French ships to impress sailors against orders, and ultimately President Madison repealed politically to favor the English supremacy.

"As Britain was admitted, generously and nobly admitted to be the soul of the confederacy, and as Mr. Madison knows this as well as we do; he affirms in his message, that the success of the British arms is favorable to our commerce is friendly to the independence and tranquility of all the world"[cxxiii]. Unfortunately for New England, they could no longer depend on the defeated French for defense. The Union's former ally, France, committed the same impressments on American vessels and was never held accountable.

The majority of politicians in the expanding country, at the time of the conspiring foreign governments, broke constitutional law by declaring war on a country not invading. As time passed, the majority expanded north, south, and west, spreading the confederacy through manipulating politicians. As expansion became the key to majority dominance, the army was sent to Canada to claim what was apparently America's land, not the original French and Indian inhabitants. As the army left, America was weak for invasion because they had declared war without any defense. England then began attacking a sitting duck.

With no army to defend, the government had to call upon the militia in every state. As New England was being invaded, the New England state residences were legitimately being called into duty by their own government. According to the Constitution at the time of an invasion, the militia was to be formed by the state and then was to be trained and led by the government.

Not only did the government control the militia, but they also controlled the lost plots of the unfortunate soldiers who could not fulfill their family purpose to pay bills, which were unable to be paid because of false compensation. As a result, soldier's wives could not maintain the property through a lower income profession. The state in which soldiers were a protecting resident no longer was responsible for compensation. After approximately thirty thousand died, "its international rights still undefined, and the expenditure of one hundred millions of dollars in The War of 1812"[cxxiv], the state no longer was the voice of the people.

New Englanders felt betrayed by the same men who once stood beside them proclaiming a newly acquired freedom. New England's production was one of the greatest assets to American commerce until manufacturing took over, which Virginia felt was rightfully their claim. The residence of New England felt that it was unfair for others outside their state to benefit from their own individual state's resources. Consequently, a separation in the nation's opinion began to marginally increase.

Kenny never listened to me when I attempted to interrupt him and get a word in, because he was confident that he knew everything about the war. He felt the war had separated the country between the Federalists and the Con-Federalists. The Con-Federalists, who continued slavery after its abolishment, also attempted to take over reign of the government through the Virginian Madison.

Kenny even brought up to me how "General Ross marched Washington (Aug. 24) and burned the capitol, the Congressional library, and other public building and records, with private dwellings and store-houses"[cxxv]. Yet, at the time I saw no relevance to what he was implicating from the 1814 events.

He was so researched on the war that he was able to quote many of the historical books he had read inside and out, in college and after. One night he let me know how "the Federalists have never studied the art of tickling the people, for they have been too intent upon doing them good, to think of that. The democratic leaders have studied to give them good words, and served them with bad fare. They have talked everything well; they have done every thing ill. They are good talkers, but poor workmen: they have much fancy, but little judgment; they have the appearance of great zeal, but they have no wisdom. They promise much, but they perform nothing"[cxxvi]. Any act, no matter how ill mannered, was manipulated through an interpretation of which "all the means of seducing the minds, are added to those of subduing the force of the people"[cxxvii].

When the guide of right for this country was altered by its very own president, the righteous felt it was necessary to address the unrepresentative acts, "Fortunately for the nation's tranquility," as Kenny continued explaining the war, "a group of delegates from all the weakened New England states attempted to dethrone Madison, and met in Hartford to discuss the inevitable destruction of their freedom."

The collective interest of the New England delegates was to, by some means end, the unfair, unjustifiable war. The New England delegates felt that the declaration of war was unconstitutional because the only justification was the impressments made by the English, which had originally been forced upon American sea vessels by Americans.

Impressments were an obvious smokescreen, because the quantity captured "on board British vessels did not exceed three hundred, yet war was still declared"[cxxviii]. The capturing of American seamen improved the power of Britain's navy, for their strength relied upon the ability of getting seamen. "They were forced against their will for bearing a flag different to England, and as the English benefited, their navy strengthened for another valuable conquer. America was fueling the stronger enemy before the French defeat"[cxxix]. The French American alliance crumbled once America could no longer depend on its defeated ally.

As I knew, yet he still had to remind me, after Napoleon fled Russia and left his men to die in Lithuania in 1812, the English and French became balanced in power. However, before French defeat, the Republicans creation of the embargo already crippled America, along with turning their cheek against the French impressments. Unfortunately, New England was crippled in many different ways than the rest of the Union.

Kenny quoted at least one political science thesis to me every time he was over to see my cousin, Jenn. One night he went on that "all the Federalists believed, not only that this was, but that it was to be, a war on the side, and in aid of, the tyrant of France; to assist him in enslaving all the powers of Christendom; and, therefore, also, they opposed it; who can deny that this was Moral"[cxxx].

New England was no longer the capital for commerce transaction in the developing America, because the province could not trade with foreign nations throughout the embargo. "Congress, from the clause in the constitution," was able "to regulate commerce with foreign nations, and among the several states and with the Indian tribes"[cxxxi]. Thus, New England became a target for the enemy and congress. New England received no revenue through commerce due to the embargo, unfortunately, making New England's currency insufficient. The immoral acts, led by a president, disabled any possibility for a strong state militia just as Henri witnessed under Hull in Detroit.

The majority of the Union justified necessity of the war by the declaration through England's impressments, yet America was unprepared for an offensive war. Why did the revolutionized legislature declare the war? Kenny once inquired to me. I told him I did not know, because I knew they only could approach the war defensively based on the known strength of the crown's navy.

Kenny explained to me that the Constitution clearly opposed the declaration of war in 1812, because there was no invasion. America was not prepared for the dominance the English power possessed and New England suffered severely due to the deceitful acts. "The ambassadors being appointed and sent, with a view to procure a peace, they were appointed and sent, with a view to make the war popular, and thus to postpone the accomplishment of peace"[cxxxii]

According to Kenny's story of his descendant, Nat protested outside the Hartford Convention in 1814 to demonstrate the disgrace of the war. Unfortunately, "the Hartford Convention was the end of the federalist party. But it had none the less been a very sinister sign of the times"[cxxxiii]. As Kenny recited all of his knowledge to me I was just as amazed with his quotes as he had been with the journal. He told me that the Convention displayed how "New England was fed up with defense of which Madison deliberately had withdrawn, and proper portion of revenue if the state was to provide her own defense"[cxxxiv].

The Hartford Convention met in 1814 to discuss any salvageable options for New England. The convention did not at one moment perform any manifestation against the government. The entire convention was recorded and performed with the utmost respect for the prosperity of the country, which initially would have been avoiding any great conflict with the English. Unfortunately, New England Federalists could not avoid the declaration of war, because it prescribed to Jefferson's plan. America, just as Europe had, gave way to the plan of continuous warfare.

One night Kenny quoted Woodrow Wilson on how "France was doing much more to injure neutral trade than England was, it was a natural but tragical accident that the war should be against England, not against France. New England had contributed men and money to the war as the law required and her means permitted. Because she was wealthy and populous, she had, indeed, contributed more than the South and West, whose representatives in Congress had brought the war on despite her passionate protests"[cxxxv].

When Kenny was drunk, quotes came out one after another, just as one night he let me know how "wars [produced] armies, debts and taxes; and as Mr. Madison said in 1795, Armies, debts and taxes are the known instruments by which the many are brought under the domination of the few"[cxxxvi].

The collection of New England delegates meeting in Hartford, to end the war, was of men whose only interest was the freedom for their own state and nation. They did not convene secretly to manipulate law. They wanted America to remain true to the regulations that composed their recently diminished freedom.

There was no other option for New England states to invoke, other than convening to resolve the unconstitutional acts performed. The convention's resolution was to inform the government of their unjust acts upon the most influential location of commerce. "The internal taxes, the land tax, license tax, stamp tax, carriage tax, sugar tax, and tax on distilleries, were hastening as fast as our worst enemies could wish, the destruction of these remote, industrious excellent counties. What enemy had spared, the protector, our own government, seizes!"[cxxxvii].

As all of New England struggled with the enemy, they became conscious that their fighting was not justifiable. The depletion of New England's commerce from the failed embargo, before the start of war, eliminated any trade with France or England, which weakened all of New England for a war yet to be declared.

Kenny told me that the war abruptly ended a few weeks after the convention began, yet as I knew little on the subject according to Kenny, the fighting continued in New Orleans January 6, 1815, led by General Jackson. After the victorious battle of New Orleans, the majority of the country somehow "obliterated the memory of many defeats"[cxxxviii] during The War of 1812. The outcome ultimately split the nation, north from south, morality from hypocritical savagery.

Kenny had only become conscious of the fabricated warfare towards natives through his studies of "General Jackson's official report to General Pinkney, of his battle with the Indians, that 'determining to exterminate them,' he detached General Coffee with the mounted men and nearly the whole of the Indian force early on the mourning of yesterday, to cross the river about two miles below their encampment, and to surround the bend in such a manner as that none of them should escape by attempting to cross the river"[cxxxix].

The Hartford Convention adjourned January 14, 1815 and was effective in addressing incorrect legislation, ultimately ending the unjust war. "The war was very unpopular to the New Englanders because of the great losses in commerce, and because they paid more than half the expense; nor had New England any sympathy with that invasion of Canada which was so popular in the West"[cxl].

"Once the system of embargo was given up by our administration, it became their unprofitable business of doing us the most harm. When our government abandoned any system of policy, it was then immediately adopted by our enemies as the most hostile to our interests which they themselves could devise"[cxli].

The freedom that the convention attempted to reestablish was impossible, especially after the conquest of Madison's cabinet. Not only was the good nature of the convention disclosed, but it was manipulated into a convention meeting with the sole interest of planning secession. The New England Federalists upset politicians demonstrating the confederate formula. This ultimately destroyed the same Federalist Party that during The War of 1812 questioned the president's decision to declare war without invasion.

Even though the end of the war was not assumed as a result of the Hartford Convention, the validity the delegates expressed was monumental to the country's true strive for freedom. However, the population south of New England felt the acts of the convention were as unconstitutional as the declaration made by Madison truly was. Mainly, the propaganda created by the interest of beneficial individuals stirred the hatred. Confederates justified the convention as a means to destroy their union's freedom.

Kenny continued that the government's arrangement, which weakened the politics within New England, broadened the separation in the United States, and The War of 1812 served as a precursor for The Civil War. "This attitude was so well understood that during the first few months of the war English cruisers had orders not to capture vessels owned in New England. As the war advanced, these orders were withdrawn and the territory of Massachusetts in the District of Maine was invaded by British troops. An urgent call for protection was then made upon the general government; but even in the crisis Massachusetts would not permit her militia to pass under the control of national military officers"[cxlii]. He then told me that not all political men were able to dispose of morals at will. The New England states stopped the war through the convention, while the southern politicians continued to demonstrate their unconstitutional and immoral acts. "The Governor of Connecticut refused to send militia, declaring that he must "yield obedience to the paramount authority of the Constitution and laws"[cxliii].

The knowledge I continuously received from Kenny was clear. He showed me how many politicians had become "illuminate for victories obtained by thousands over hundreds, and then call generals who achieve such victories heroes"[cxliv]. The politicians only chose such acts during The War of 1812 because they had "the desire to acquire the outlet of the St. Lawrence, and to rob the Indians of their lands, and to erect a standing army, and to increase the power and patronage of the president, were the secret motives to this contest"[cxlv].

However, "the causes of the war, as set forth in the messages of the President and in contemporary speeches, were four. The first was that the British had tampered with the Indians and urged them to hostilities: it was true, and it was trying; but the breaking out of war simply aggravated that difficulty. The second charge was the interference with neutral trade by the Orders in Council; but the injury from the French Decrees had been more humiliating. The third complaint was perhaps the most serious and exasperating: it was the virtual blockade of American ports by British cruisers, and their interference with arriving and departing vessels. Finally came the impressment of American seamen"[cxlvi].

Thus, "the disaffection of the Federalists was publicly expressed by Josiah Quincy, of Massachusetts, in a speech in 1811 on the admission of Louisiana: "If this bill passes, it is my deliberate opinion that it is virtually a dissolution of this Union; that it wall free the States from their moral obligation; and, as it will be the right of all, so it will be the duty of some, definitely to prepare for a separation, amicably if they can, violently if they must. "

Nor did the military and naval preparation of the country make up for its political weakness. The regular army of the United States was composed of 6,700 men. The service was so unpopular that two proclamations were issued in 1812 promising pardons to deserters. The highest number of officers and men in the regular army was during the war but 34,000. The dependence of the government, therefore, for offensive operations was upon the State militia. The general officers were old Revolutionary soldiers or men who had seen no service; the military organization was defective; and the Secretary of War, Eustis, was incompetent. In naval affairs, the American navy consisted of twelve vessels, the largest of which were the three 44 gun frigates "United States," "Constitution," and "President." The number of men was 4,000, with 1,500 marines. The British navy was composed of eight hundred and thirty vessels, of which two hundred and thirty were larger than any of the American ships; they had 150,000 seamen, and unlimited power of impressing sailors"[cxlvii].

Nat Carter was connected to the ramifications at the time of the war as he delivered papers for the Hartford Times after his period of slavery. In agony on his deathbed in 1852, he shared that "the future condition of the colored race in this country will be the question overmastering all others for many years to come. The slave aristocracy controls the south. As slavery called this aristocracy into being, and created its power, so it holds it in being; anything which strikes at slavery strikes at the root of its power. And, therefore, slavery will never be given voluntarily up. Only irresistible force will extinguish it: It will die only as it is killed"[cxlviii]. Nat knew the people up north were modified to the Constitution, unlike the slave owning southern majority. Through the depleted Federalist's in Hartford, Nat became educated on his free right and on the men who took it. Kenny had one piece of paper written from his descendant that provided me with hope:

"Remember, that although one set of men have been able to drive the nation down, from the high elevation of prosperity it had reached under other; remember, that the mad rulers, who seem now bent on destroying everything that is left; are not immortal; remember too, that although an honest, a patriotic, and intelligent people may be deluded, and that although even when the delusion is dissipate, even when they begin to see, and to see clearly too, with the eyes of their own understandings, they may, from pride, delay the acknowledgment of their convictions, yet no people ever had, or ever can have, a motive powerful enough; to make them the voluntary victims of unmerited and unnecessary sufferings; of self inflicted, but unavailing torture"[cxlix].

After discussing The War of 1812, Kenny had knowledge on any other topic I would mention, except King Phillip's War or any other type of Native American history beside Jackson's campaign of annihilation. He knew a lot about the slave trade, and did not realize until I told him that it also was demonstrated on Native Americans. He told me that the English colonists were the founding fathers of the confederate practices, which included slavery. The first legitimacy of slavery took place in Virginia in 1606. Without the educated knowledge Kenny obtained, I questioned the factual knowledge he brought up on slavery because I never heard of most of the subjects his ancestry and education dealt with.

After Kenny took out his hundreds of notes, diaries, and newspaper articles from the nineteenth century that helped him earn his degree, I believed all Kenneth Carter said. "This is what made enslaving another man just," explained Kenny after allowing me to browse the articles of proof. He handed me the article that justified slavery. The First Virginia Charter, written April 10, 1606: "Wee, Greately commending and graciously accepting of theire desires to the furtherance of soe noble a worke which may, by the providence of Almighty God, hereafter tende to the glorie of his divine majestie in propagating of Christian religion suche people as yet live in darkenesse and miserable ignorance of the true knowledge and worshippe of God and may in tyme bring the infidels and salvages living in those parts to humane civilite and to a settled and quiet governmente, doe by theise our letters patents graciously accepte of and agree to theire humble and well intended desires"[cl].

After four years of college, Kenny felt the paradox of slavery lied in Africa, the nation that also defined the infinite light of Christianity through St. Augustine. However, proceeding St. Augustine and the dark ages, Africa became the destination for the rightful enslavement of free man through God's will. Both Christianity and slavery were formed in the same nation that exported both slaves and the eternal faith.

One drunken night, Kenny went on about St. Augustine to me. He was born in Africa and had a great influence on Christian philosophy. He did not follow the philosophers before him in explaining all eternal elements in the universe. His work was based on justifying Christianity.

"Thus by making Being, rather than Unity and Goodness, the basis of his account of God, he supplemented the Aristotelian and Plutonian traditions, with their many inadequacies, and wrote of a God, at once immanent and transcendent, super-eminent in Being, but the Creator of a universe that reflected his perfections, and the provident and loving ruler and Father of His children"[cli].

As few prominent influencers of Christianity have done, St Augustine used in theory many similar principles of the founding philosophers, which seemed to dialect most truths in the universe. Unfortunately after St. Augustine's time, "The teacher of the law for had taken away the key of knowledge; the right of free discussion"[clii]. St. Augustine took some of the defining philosophy and put it into his own Christian theory. As the true nature of a balanced universe left with the arrival of slavery and genocide, immoral comprehension formed through misinterpretations. "From about A.D. 350 till about A.D. 500 the vital powers of the ancient civilization were steadily declining, while at the same time the Church was coming to social maturity with a number of insistent needs and demands which had not made themselves felt until full freedom of action had been attained". Augustine was one of the few to teach others "to absorb the message of the ancient world while it was still to be heard"[cliii].

As time passed, theory had been configured through expansion, reversing the true growth that naturally formed the universe of God in and out of ones self. Kenny said "Acts towards others should unite eternal nature with mortal man to preserve our light of day. Yet with the dark ages the overcompensation of immorality created an inevitability of wrong. The threat of breaking bureaucratic theory had forced wrong into right."

Kenny learned there was little idea of an eternal soul by the founding philosophers, instead dialect of a "world soul" [cliv] formed by abiding to universal nature. St. Augustine's African education strengthened his eternal concept for Christianity. However, with the theory and forgiveness of religion, the philosophy of the truth available to everyone seemed impossible to connect with, shaping the Dark Ages.

Chapter 8

Racketeering

One night while Kenny and I were in Jenn's apartment without her there, Kenny got real drunk and all of his deep revelations came out. The more Kenny drank from the bottle, the more he began to deeply talk to me about his knowledge. He felt the departure from free discussion changed philosophy into religion. Men who ignored the theories of reality that demonstrated the balance of harmony hid the universal truths philosophy established. Misinterpretation had become, as the configured dialectic of philosophy became, one distinction.

Kenny imbedded in me that "the same Savages, Madison defined as slaves, were predisposed to slavery, only because of the control his theory on God's will established upon Americans."

"Wait," I interrupted, "Native Americans were also considered savages even after colonists only allowed Indians to join their crusade by means of becoming a Christian. Indians were enslaved because the theory of justice formed wrong into right. Indians, unfortunately, became enslaved to enrich commerce. Even though many Indian tribes were just as much of a believer in Christ as Christians, the settlers did not except any other creed."

Kenny, not wanting to get outsmarted by a high school graduate, revealed through his education that the African traditions passed on through slavery became lost, just as my Native American traditions were. He told me that the lost traditions felt God came in every form of action. The light of God was eternal to all living. As with Christians, "It is the created light of the sun, 'illuminated' for the minds perception by a divine light. The light is the one intellectualizing element in the whole of creation, reflecting the uncreated light of God." Kenny's "knowledge," as St. Augustine, was based on "the supreme, immutable Truth by intuition"[clv].

The lost tribes had also celebrated the eternal light of nature, yet the conquerors apparently did not see the same nourishing light. The deceit that the Indians withstood symbolized the loss of divinity in human nature. As immoral colonists were forgiven through Christian theory, the wrong authority expanded and exterminated at will.

After the drunken religious talk with him, I had enough. Kenny reminded me way too much of my father, yet not as depressing. Also, he always spoke to me with great urgency. All I needed was a quick break from Kenny. However, the next time we met up at the club he sold his drugs out of, he asked me if I would move in with him. I was all about living with an entertaining guy and not my female cousin. The two of us took a shot to celebrate the confirmation. Then Kenny started up again. He said, "My descendant, Nat Carter, could not handle being enslaved under a theory by a state in the Union, even though it was unlawful by 1808. The enraged assembly of slaves, antagonized by Nat, first traveled to Philadelphia where the first abolitionist society was founded in 1775. However, Nat felt the overwhelming turmoil in Philadelphia, and headed north."

The legendary Carter story was told many times to me as we began living together and it actually helped me create a kinship for democracy, even though my father would never have agreed with it. The discoveries I made through Kenny's knowledge, which recognized New England's acceptance of runaway slaves, the Federalist Party and the Hartford Convention, defused all my anger towards all New Englanders. I realized that under military order nothing could be avoided, just as my father proved to me that the English were responsible for the destruction of the many surrendered tribes. Kenny was very informed of his ancestry just as I was and tried to share everything he knew with his new friend.

I moved in with Kenny once he had trouble paying the rent, which I easily contributed to once he got me on a Jai Alai team. He knew I was good because I always showed off my skills to him in the back ally of the strip club. Moving in with Kenny was not the greatest atmosphere for an evolving athlete, but it was better than living with my female cousin. Unfortunately for me, Kenny Carter dealt with many drugs and was not faithful to my cousin.

He initially told me when I moved in, "1 know everything and I'm the best at everything. Do not question me."

Drug dealing was no exception. He dealt with and used every substance, and like my brother, Mark, drugs ruined his athletic dream. According to Kenny, a new drug phenomenon and gambling ruined his success. The ditch was dug once he got cut from the Knicks.

Failure was inevitable for him, because he could not recognize true success. Kenny joined his lifelong friend, Dan Dellski's, illegitimate operation his senior year in college. Once Kenny flawed a game in college for his own benefit, his potential became lost.

I compared Kenny's strife his senior year in college to Mark's expulsion his senior year in high school, because their poor decisions were influenced by drugs. Unfortunately for my brother, he became ruined for a second time in Boston. This was the result of the same phenomenon that ruined Kenny in New York.

Mark, after falling into an impossible debt in Boston, visited me in Hartford "to surprise his ambitious younger brother." Unfortunately, my mother called Mark from Ohio and excitingly told her eldest how I made a team within a month of arriving in Hartford. Mark got my new address from Jenn on the phone, after I moved in with Kenny, and then immediately left Boston.

When Mark first arrived in Hartford and walked into our apartment, his first glimpse at his younger brother was of me dealing Kenny's drugs to our neighbors. Mark was very surprised and could not believe his athletically dedicated brother's new occupation.

By that time, I was helping Kenny sell his drugs to pay the rent for our apartment. I made sure not to use any of the substances, while Kenny was away dealing at the silver club. I made one hundred percent profit.

After the two of us Adams hugged and caught up, I turned to my brother and said, "If you can't beat them join them, right." My first month in the Jai Alai circuit had taught me a lot about earning money. At first, I had great difficulty performing with little playing time. Yet, after the house bookie as well as Reggie's best friend, Ski (Dan Dellski), educated me, I became noticed.

The best thing for my Jai Alai career was when Kenny got me a tryout a week after we first met. He understood how I felt because I told him my dream the moment we met. Kenny then told his childhood friend that he met a solid player, because he watched me play against an ally wall. Ski made arrangements with me for a tryout in front of the president of World Jai Alai, Hal Coffey.

"Ski" was the only name I acknowledged, the man who helped me excel in Jai Alai. The under six foot, three hundred pound stocky Polack, was Kenny's only bookie and friend before me. Ski was also his best drug connection. Ski knew everything about everyone involved with either gambling or drugs in Hartford County.

Ski told me after my first week of struggling with Jai Alai "not to worry about being your best, if you mess up for me, others will mess up for you." To say the least, I quickly became a star benefiting from Ski's advice. The corruption I inter-meshed quickly gained me the salary of a star. The popularity of the newly established gambling fix influenced many addicts in Hartford. The first month went perfect for me with Kenny and Ski by my side, until Mark showed up in 1980.

Mark, unfortunately, could not break even in life or with his affiliated gang in Boston, who spotted him all his drug invest-ments. The most powerful gang in Boston loaned more and more drugs to Mark without any return. The Irish Summer Hill Gang controlled most illegal transaction with little interruption in Boston.

I knew Mark fell in debt because of an uncontrollable addiction, even though he told our mother that he needed money because his friends would not give him the money they owed him for rent. After having his life threatened for the thir-ty thousand dollars he owed the gang, Mark left Boston. He quickly manifested a jealousy of my success and chose to check it out in Hartford.

As Mark first walked in our apartment and saw his brother's operation, he wanted an in to my successful illegitimacy. After the buyers cleared out, I told Mark everything that had happened to me in Hartford. I finished the story by telling my older brother that he could absolutely not be involved in or say anything about it. I did not even tell my roommate Kenny. He was Ski's best friend, yet he knew nothing of the Jai Alai scam because of Ski's threats to the participating players, especially me.

All Kenny and Ski did together was smoke and talk about basketball lines. Kenneth Carter, ironically, was not the best at one lone thing, gambling. He always made an initial profit from drug dealing, yet all of his profit (aside from rent and food), went to Ski to pay off the gambling debt he continued to accumulate. After he got cut from the Knicks for doing too many drugs, Kenny had no motivation to use his degree and thought if he used his NBA salary to gamble on the team that cut him he would earn quick money and never have to work again.

After being drafted by the Knicks and participating in forty games his rookie season, he did not recognize the effects of drugs until he was cut. Yet, Kenny still felt he had a special connection to the team, after spending almost a year with them. He always took them with or against the points. It did not matter, the 1981 season cost Kenny Carter ten thousand dollars. Luckily for Kenny, at the time of his betting, Ski was his bookie. Ski and Kenny grew up together, and Ski owed all his success to Kenny.

Ski not only made money on the drugs he gave Kenny to sell, but his greatest profit came from the basketball player who never could rid his ten thousand dollar gambling debt. Kenny's biggest problem was that he felt gambling was the only avenue to connect him with basketball. He continued to gamble on the Knicks until the day he died.

Ski made a lot of money without any problem, until trouble began when Kenny and Ski arrived outside our apartment from a rewarding night at the Silver Club. It was the night when Mark first arrived in Hartford. The pair overheard Mark and me inside the apartment. While they stood outside the door they could hear Mark boasting. As Mark smoked a blunt, he began pleading with his successful younger brother; Ski and Kenny heard everything outside the door.

Mark took a couple drags, he then stood up and blurted out, "Pat, I've lived and learned, I want in with you and Ski. I can bring you and me a lot of money because I can connect infinite money to your Jai Alai game." Consequently, Ski quickly slammed open the door after Mark's boasting, sprinted over punched Mark, and then grabbed my neck while spitting in my face.

Ski screamed at me an inch away from my face, "You and your brother are going to be killed tonight."

Mark, attempting to interrupt our murders, then told Ski, "I obviously would not blurt something out like that if I was only in it for myself. I know a connection that could bring us millions."

Because of the respect he had for me Ski let me go and then told Mark to continue. Mainly he let us go because Ski liked how a million dollars sounded. Ski allowed Mark to talk about his scheme, he began by telling us all about his stay in Boson, and created the fib on how his downfall stemmed from his inability to ask others for (drug) money that was rightfully his. He created the fib to the three of us now sitting, even though I knew the truth, Mark explained, "I did not like telling the gang about the increasing debt I had made because they had murdered for debts of only fifteen dollars."

He continued on with his unfortunate time in Boston, "As the loans increased to pay off the growing debt, the debt increased to pay off the growing loan. I was getting threatened everyday and had no out to the debt or gang." He really did not have any other option than leaving Boston. According to Mark, the petty pot debts he had forced upon himself because of stingy friends no longer was small. Mark was then forced by the gang to pay off the pot debt by selling other drugs he did not use. The gang would receive a greater profit if Mark did not use the gang's supply.

Unfortunately, as the assortment of drugs increased, Mark's experimentation increased. Mark's intrigue turned into fascination, he could not climb out of the deep ditch he had fallen into. Mark said his life "seemed to become a contest of who could get messed up off the most intense substance." Mark fell into a much worse drug habit than our father, who was only a drunken stoner.

Chief Russell used pot and booze, because he felt they strengthened the spirit. He did not smoke cigarettes because of the evil tobacco brought to others. His father, however, made all his riches due to the greed from the most artificial drug created. Chief Russell felt pot was not nearly as addictive as nicotine, and it was natural not chemically enhanced. He felt pot grew from the same photosynthesis as trees, imperative for earth's survival, unlike the sticks made to strengthen addiction.

Russell told me, a month before his fall, that true nature was destroyed rapidly for a calculation of expense. Expansion had no concern for the environment or future according to my father, Russell. Somehow, self interested Americans felt for the promotion of America it was necessary to take fellow American's rightful land for industrial benefit.

Unlike Mark, Chief Russell had somewhat succeeded the illegitimate way through selling drugs, but it was from his own homegrown pot. The chief sold the farm's crop in ounces, which were bought by the dozen. It was the same pot which Mark, his childhood neighbor, and best friend Tommy got kicked off their basketball team for.

Mark, unfortunately, did not realize that the debt he had monopolized with the Summer Hill gang was due to our father's influence of drugs. All Mark wanted was to smoke for free as his father always boasted drunkenly about when he said, "Not only do I get high for and with others, but I do it for free."

Members of the depleted Indian tribes, who Grandpa Herbert reassembled and my father entertained, lived throughout New England and Canada. This allowed Chief Russell's pot crops to earn back his little invested money. He did not make any profit, just enough to pay the bills, get drunk, and smoke for free. He only sold his crops to fellow Indians. Unfortunately for my brother, Russell did not care if Mark pinched off the crop at his own leisure.

My father told Mark that he smoked his first pipe with a descendant of the same Nipmuck tribe whom Eluwilussit belonged to. Our Grandfather Herbert knew what his son did when Russell was fifteen at a powwow, yet Herbert did not condemn it. He allowed Russell to have continued affiliation with the tribe, hoping that his son would take advantage of his cultural obligations.

Years later, one night, Chief Russell regretfully told Mark, that he had smoked and grew pot. At first, Mark did not believe him, because he thought his father only dealt with nicotine as his grandfather had. Yet, a month after the eleven year old was told by Russell that he smoked pot, he saw his father hide away in the haunted barn; Mark followed him...

After the chief's justification and sharing of pot, Mark became hooked. Pot, as well as many other profitable resources of the natives, was considered normal in society when colonists depended on Indians for survival. Yet, once the association with praying Indians ended based on the magnified savagery by the rebellious Indians, the native herb, theorized by colonists, was considered an influence of deviance.

I, on the other hand, thought like my mother did about pot. She knew it was wrong because she witnessed first hand the disturbances it had caused. That is also what my teacher taught to me in a Pittsfield Elementary School after she heard stories about my father. Yet, I was well misunderstood about pot, according to Mark. Fortunately, I never believed my brother, especially after Mark blamed voices for his deviant act against our father, when he was seventeen and showed me the Jai Alai sticks for the first time. My brother was never the same after the beating he received from our father. The first misconception that I held, according to Mark, was that pot caused harm toward others.

The chief disclosed to Mark, the first time they smoked together, that he did not get high for himself. "Pot brought a spiritual revelation to my Native American soul," spattered the chief only to his eldest, who later told me. The main reason the chief continued to distribute marijuana, while making it just, was his rationale of distributing joy into others that did not use the substance through others who used it.

The night that the chief disclosed his illegal crop and habit to Mark was immensely impacting. The chief told Mark that pot helped him motivate his own intellect. As some Indians used pot to grasp the stillness of nature, the colonists used pot to symbolize acts of a demon or witch.

After Ski and Kenny took in Mark's life story, Ski told us Adams to relax and then we smoked. Kenny told Ski that he had no idea about the scheme and then had to prove a point. Yet again, he went on about his opinion on something. This time marijuana, and continued the conversation Mark began on drugs. At that time, Kenny agreed with the rationalization of illegal narcotics. If he had not been arrested for possession right before he got kicked off the Knicks, he would probably have overdosed off the amount he was planning on ingesting.

Kenny felt the government would profit immensely from controlling legalization, because violence and debts would reduce greatly. He realistically thought it would work if the purchasers would be punished severely for sharing the substance to minors. Somehow, Kenny then came up with a response that made no sense to the three of us. "Pot was one example that demonstrated the distance of the true philosophical theories from the theories of individual thinking."

He did not stop after that, which made my brother and me very thankful to have the attention off of us. He went on about how the first theorists, who were also the founding philosophers, dealt with all dimensions of the universe. Kenny felt the eternal elements created both universe and man, displaying the eternal God in everything. Consequently, the inability to differentiate true justice from immorality, manufactured through individual theory, destroyed equal justice. As theory drifted away from sharing logic, religion went from dialect of the founding philosophers to opinions of theorists. After the unenlightened Dark Ages occurred and showed what happens with the manipulation of morals, justice was formed by individual theory.

Mark had trouble listening to Kenny, because he only believed everything his father told him until the fall. Mark came to the realization that his heritage was of no concern when he left to Boston with Tommy and other childhood friends. They intended to score big with his money from a third of the farm. Just as I decided to leave after I saw our father fall, Mark decided to exile from his father's lifestyle. Mark then entered into the land of amphetamine during his time in Boston.

There was no longer anyone around to smoke with or talk to in Boston. Mark got caught in the hypocrisy of which the chief always professed. Mark now chose to use unnatural substances to believe in the natural spirit. Mark never did anything right, especially once he left Pittsfield for Boston. However, in Hartford I made great connections without drug use, opposite of my brother in the depopulated Pittsfield, and then Boston. I did not want to continue my father's low earnings.

When Mark came in debt to the largest gang in New England, he headed, never looking back, to Hartford. Mark did not have any idea on his trip down to Hartford that he would be back in Boston the following week. Somehow, after having his life threatened, Mark then convinced Ski that the Summer Hill Gang would invest profitable interest in Jai Alai if his petty fixings were shared with them.

Due to my impressive financial results for Ski, he considered negotiating a much greater partnership with my older brother, which he assumed would bring in an infinite profit. Yet, he was still not impressed with how Mark first presented himself.

I explained to Ski, on my brother's behalf, that he should not mind his uncontrollable nature, because he has schizophrenia. I did not know what Ski intended to do and all I could wish for was that Mark's life and my life would be spared, to have the ability to continue to participate in the live gambled sport, and to continue using Ski's drugs and position to make money.

I, unlike my brother, discovered the enormous profit of drugs through my cousin's relationship with Kenny. I never once thought about touching or selling drugs in Pittsfield. The moment when I saw how influential he was, I gave in and wanted what Reggie had created. Not only was Reggie the first person who smoked with me, but he was also the link that connected me to the stardom I had received because of Jai Alai. Because of fixing the game I loved, fame and money poured in. I was also making a killing from selling Kenny's drugs. Fortunately for me, Kenny was not only the boyfriend of my cousin, but he was also the best friend of the only bookie in the Hartford Jai Alai circuit.

Chapter 9
Dan Dellski

Kenny knew Dan Dellski since nursery school and the two opposites quickly began an immeasurable friendship after playing blocks. A lot had happened between the two since nursery school. When Kenny was twelve, his parents died in a fire, and the Dellski family took the orphan in.

Kenny, consequently, owed his basketball ability to Ski. Dan was the only one who motivated the six foot five fifteen year old to play basketball everyday. Ski did not want to see his huge best friend not live up to his potential. Mainly, Dan loved basketball more than his best friend but was too short and heavy to be effective, unlike the lanky and athletic Kenny.

After receiving a full scholarship through his stellar career at Hartford High, Kenny left the south end of Hartford for the west end to attend college. After Kenny left his adopted home, Dan began to gamble and sell drugs to fill the everyday void Kenny had filled and that is when he became known as Ski. Ski had no other options, the only reason he attended and graduated high school was due to the fame he received everyday, which Kenny brought to his fat unpopular best friend.

Otherwise, Ski would have dropped out and depended on his gambling ability, which won at least 75 percent of the time.

Ski felt as if he was invincible and never wanted to get out. After Kenny's departure to college, drug addicts who hung out at the same places as unemployed successful gamblers influenced Ski. However, Ski never took the drugs. He just began supplying them. Drugs separated the two best friends at first. Kenny's energy during college was entirely directed to basketball, until partying the beginning of his senior year took precedent.

He was all conference for the University of West Hartford his junior year and began his senior year with just expectations. His work ethic was incomparable to any teammate, in large part to Ski's continuing dedication to motivate Kenny. Even though he moved out of Dan's house, the two still had trained five times a week during the off season throughout Kenny's college career.

Ski's dedication to gambling and drug dealing paralleled Kenny's overall motivation towards basketball in college. After Kenny left Ski's house for college, Ski had an enormous amount of time, which was spent mainly hanging out with hoodlums and occasionally with Kenny during his free time in college. Ski started hanging around with other eighteen year old townies who wanted a fast life, yet none of them brought the women that Ken could.

Ski quickly got his name out there to all the south end gamblers and addicts. He befriended the neighborhood drug connection at a party while Kenny was on a road game his freshman year. After obtaining a large amount of drugs from his gambling commission, he told Kenny about his score, when he returned from a road game. Ski told Kenny to tell his roommate and team about his products. With Kenny's networking Ski ran drugs and spreads throughout the college.

However, Kenny never chose to use Ski's services until his senior season. Unfortunately for Kenny, his climaxing college popularity got the best of him fall semester, right before his senior basketball season. He partied every night with women, Ski, and the gang of Ski's underworld friends. Kenny had his own apartment for the first time his final collegiate season, however he only could maintain rent with assistance from Ski. Consequently, Kenny still needed more money to party it up.

Reggie was positive that in the opening game of his senior season West Hartford would beat Central Connecticut by more than the twelve point spread. Kenny needed more money to pay rent for his off campus place because he spent his little money on booze and girls. He figured the hundred dollar bet with his best friend, the petty bookie, was easy money. Ski was all about the implications, and also bet the most he ever had. He placed a grand of his own money on Kenny's sure thing. Kenny did his part to help the cause, scoring thirty and grabbing ten boards. The University of West Hartford won by twenty five.

With the first attempt being successful, the two wanted more easy money. Sadly, the money was so easy that Kenny lost games to earn a couple thousand dollars extra, which he blew on girls and booze. Luckily for Kenny, he salvaged his degree only because of the three four he brought into his one three senior year.

As the money increased with framing both wins and losses, Kenny did not mind missing a lay up to lose by seven to Uconn, instead of six. At the time, he did not realize his poor performance hindered his once promising draft position. Consequently, Kenny's once athletically motivated best friend quickly only supported the drug dealing and gambling Kenny positively influenced. Both instantly became so blind that they forgot about the effort, which allowed them to peak financially. The only negative that came with winning a lot of money was that the more you take the more is wanted back. Especially, in Ski's case, when it came to under the table gambling.

Ski made an eight thousand dollar bet on the Uconn game for himself, and Kenny bet two thousand through him.

Unfortunately, no one had ever made a bet on that type of regular season college game with Billy the breaker, Ski's only bookie. Bill worked with Ski's father at Colt Firearms and he first began trading spreads with Ski in return for drugs. Ski was very comfortable with Billy after they had a long conversation about basketball and easy money when Billy was over the Dellski house.

Bill was no big time bookie but he did have a very intimidating name. He received it after breaking his nephew's knees due to a changed bet made during the first quarter of Super Bowl Thirteen. Bill was very connected to the underworld through his family. He had the ability to make any bet until an hour before a game.

For the first time since Ski began betting on The University of West Hartford with Billy, he was finally confronted about his consistent success. Billy confronted Ski at the time of payment after the Uconn win. Billy told Ski that he could not take bets with him any longer, and then gave him the ten thousand Billy's uncle owed Ski. Billy's uncle was not happy because he had lost a substantial amount of money due to a mediocre team's season. Billy told Ski no hard feelings, and gave him his uncle's address if he still wanted to gamble.

Ski loved to network and wanted to become respected by all. He easily decided to visit Bill's uncle at the address. He owned the brand new Silver Club and Ski chose to go there by himself. When Ski walked into the newly built club, the bouncer stopped him. Ski told the bouncer that Billy sent him to see the "boss." The bouncer then pointed to a man in an entire black suit with sunglasses on, even though it was midnight. Ski introduced himself and the man told Ski just to call him the boss. Ski asked the boss if he could make a wager on the next University of West Hartford home game verses the underdog the University of Buffalo. This time he was going to take

Buffalo with the three points. Kenny was not confident against their solid upstate New York rival and decided he was, again, going to have an off night.

Not only did Kenny not make a shot, but also he fouled out in the first half. Ski won ten thousand dollars, and brought an enormous amount of attention upon himself and Kenny from the gambling underworld of Hartford after the Buffalo win.

Not only did the twenty year old, Ski, have a gun immediately pointed to his head when he went to receive their winnings at the club, but he was forced at gunpoint by the boss down the stairs. Ski thought he was going to be killed and did not receive his money from the scheme at first. The boss never disclosed his name to Ski while he interrogated the scared bookie.

The boss, after sitting Ski down in the basement, wanted to know how Ski easily won over ten thousand dollars of his money betting on a semi par college basketball team's entire season. With a gun still pointed to his temple, Ski gave up the entire scam. After the boss absorbed the scenario, he wanted in on the next game. As Ski had no problem sharing the scheme, the boss patted him on the back and then handed Ski his well deserved money.

Ski decided not to tell Kenny about the boss's interest in the game. Consequently, the usual successful outcome took place with the next game against the underdog, New Hampshire, and Ski received a ten thousand dollar bonus just for the tip that won the boss over a hundred grand. Ski continued tipping the boss only for victories, because Kenny had become very aware of his poor play by his disappointed teammates and coach.

After a couple more fixed games, Kenny did not want to affect his draft status any worse and told Ski that he no longer would fix games. Kenny did not realize that he had already dropped to the second round according to scouts, mainly due to his poor performance against Uconn.

Ski understood, but was afraid to tell the boss. After a West Hartford loss, he finally mustered up the courage, he went and told the boss after ignoring him for three games. He told the boss that Kenny could no longer fix games because it would endanger his draft status. The boss had no problem with the decision, as he was already very satisfied with his winnings because of Kenny. He then rewarded Ski with the best clientele for any bookie in Hartford. The connection with the boss allowed Ski to network drugs and bets to anyone in Hartford through the Silver Club.

It seemed that everyone was connected to illegitimacy in Hartford somehow, which became obvious to Ski under the control of the boss. Ski met the most important men in Hartford at the boss's club.

One night in 1976, Ski met the man who would make him a million in a year. The owner of the entire Jai Alai Association, who became a regular at the club after prospecting Hartford as a location for his franchise, was discussing his motives with a Hartford police sergeant at the clubs bar when Ski first overheard him. Ski, always networking, overheard their discussion about the possible revenue Jai Alai would bring and wanted in.

The president of the entire World Jai Alai circuit, Hal, was new in town from Florida. "In the early 1970's, the Jai Alai industry was trying to move north from its base in Florida. Connecticut became the first northern state to legalize gambling on jai alai, the fast paced Basque game, and in 1976, World Jai Alai was seeking a license to open a fronton in Hartford"[clvi]. Hal was very successful, especially because of his mob ties.

President Hal Coffey was looking for a trustworthy bookie and asked the boss if he could share a hand. The boss had pointed out Ski to Hal as the best bookie around. After the two began talking, Ski was in. Ski explained the entire University of

West Hartford scheme, which Hal felt was the perfect experience for Jai Alai fixing. Hal introduced Ski to Sergeant Kendall, and told Ski that if he ever had trouble performing his job that the Sergeant would make sure everything went correctly.

By 1982, Hartford Jai Alai was Connecticut's greatest attraction and source of revenue. Its greatest success was happening right after my arrival. The scheme was working too perfectly. Not too many people were involved in the Jai Alai fixing, until Mark arrived.

As Ski enjoyed Mark's ability to bring in substantial revenue through his gang connections, he still had to bring the idea to Hal. At first Hal did not want to listen, but once he heard the Summer Hill Gang, he gave his full attention. Hal "was a bear like man with a bottomless wallet who could be found with a table full of gangsters at the Play boy Club"[clvii]. Three days after meeting Mark, Hal joined him in Boston to discuss the possibility of expanding Jai Alai gambling with the Summer Hill leaders.

Hal met two of the most powerful gang leaders in New England, Flint and Patricks, who were very interested in investing in the scam. Mark had a smile on his face throughout the meeting he set up. The leaders gave Hal a fifty thousand dollar briefcase of Summer Hill's illegitimate money and asked him to make them a profit. The Summer Hill leaders told Mark that if he made their investment work, his debts would be cleared.

During their first month in the scheme, the Summer Hill gang profited favorably. Mark finally became successful with something, mainly because all he had to do was drive a briefcase to and from Boston. Yet, after a couple of years the "siphoning of millions out of the Jai Alai industry"[clviii] became very obvious.

The ethical vice president had not noticed the scam, until the gang won consistent substantial amounts. The vice president of Jai Alai was the only man not committing any corruption in the sport and that is why he discovered the decrease in profit. Vice President Riley, after noticing a decrease in profit, called the FBI hoping that the crookedness of Jai Alai would halt.

Riley did not realize that the FBI had sent an agent that had already been corrupted. They sent Agent Jack Palmer, who was in the FBI for twelve years, and had been "developing a reputation as the Boston FBI's pre-eminent organized crime investigator"[clix].

Not only had Palmer been from Boston, but he also had a relationship with the Summer Hill leaders. Summer Hill "gangsters provided [Palmer] with the leads he used to lock up Italian Mafia members who competed with [Summer] Hill for control of Boston's rackets"[clx].

Jack Palmer met with Hal privately, which the Summer Hill founders set up after three enormous money exchanges. Palmer told Hal that he would go to jail if he did not compensate the FBI agent for ignoring the illegal activity. Hal had no problems sharing some of his infinite earnings with the crooked cop to continue the corruption without any suspicion.

Through the business obligations of Riley, who did not record any positive change, Palmer received weekly phone calls from the suspicious vice president. Palmer told Hal, and the other Summer Hill contributors, that the problem had to be eliminated.

Hal told everyone involved that they could not harm Riley, who was his brother in-law. He told the Summer Hill leaders that the entire scheme would be called off if any blood was shed. The family relationship did not matter to the profiting gangsters once the scheme was in jeopardy. The Summer Hill gang had someone take care of the disgusted Riley. He was "shot point blank in the face"[clxi] after he finished a round of golf at Goodwin Park.

This act made Hal very angry and he made the legitimate feds gaze deeper into Palmer's investigation. Unfortunately, his investigation led right to Hal, because he was the president.

After intense interrogation, Hal remained innocent, even though the president rose or fell with the results of the regime. Without Riley, the feds did not have a solid case. As police questioned everyone associated with the Hartford Jai Alai, the Summer Hill gang became very paranoid that someone would reveal the entirety of the scheme.

Consequently, the police received the bookwork from Riley through a search warrant of Hal's office. Hal did not have any option but to tell all to save himself. He did not realize that the worst thing that someone could do in the world was snitch, according to the Summer Hill leaders. Once Palmer discovered his coworkers broke Hal in interrogation, he quickly got a hold of his Summer Hill associates.

The gang bangers had to clean their mess up to avoid prison and gave the job to the one that first got them in the Jai Alai mess, Mark. He never shot a gun before, and had no intentions of shooting Hal, who had greatly befriended me. Yet, the Summer Hill leaders and Palmer became very paranoid of becoming indicted. They reminded my brother of his debt and, also of the poor judgment that got the gang involved in the dysfunctional situation. Mark had no other option but to murder Hal.

It was difficult for Mark to touch a gun, let alone shoot it. After the Summer Hill leaders met with agent Palmer, the plan for Mark was to follow Hal after he left his home in his Cadillac, until he reached his certain destination. As Hal got out of his car, Mark was to shoot him, and then quickly place the body in the trunk of the stolen car and dump him in a trash compactor. Yet, there were a couple problems with the plan. Mark stole a flashy mint Camaro and did not want to ruin it, and also he did not know where Hal was going.

Mark followed Hal from his home in Farmington to Bradley Airport. Hal intended to fly back to Florida after ratting out the members of the largest gang in the area. Fortunately for Mark, he caught Hal right before he left for good. In 1982, Mark Adams assassinated Hal Coffey. Hal "was shot twice in the head and stuffed into the trunk of his Cadillac. The killer left a dime on [Coffey's] chest, an underworld warning to anyone who might be thinking of dropping a dime"[clxii] .

Hal was found at Bradley International Airport in the trunk of his bloody Cadillac, because Mark did not want to get his stolen car bloody. After the many eyewitnesses, answers were sought. As the blood and the body were discovered, arrests were inevitable. Everyone involved with Hartford Jai Alai was assumed to be involved with the corrupt president's murder until questioned.

I was one of the first to be interviewed because I was a player and Mark's brother, yet I did not reveal anything. Ski was never questioned, only because Hal loved Ski for his loyalty and kept no proof of his enormous illegitimate connection. Ski made him a lot of money, and did not ask him for much in return unlike the gangsters and the FBI.

Mark, on the other hand, got arrested because of the five eyewitnesses who saw that he shot a man in clear daylight and stuffed the dead body in the Cadillac, then scurried away in his flashy camaro. The police saw the stolen car the same day of the murder and the officers picked him up. Mark ended up ratting out all the guilty Summer Hill participants except Palmer, because I took his advice. I had been told by the crooked fed that if Mark avoided telling the feds Palmer's role in planning the murder of the president of Jai Alai, my brother's sentence would greatly be reduced

With Palmer's federal position, he forced the Summer Hill gang, solely, into the responsibility for Hal's murder and the Jai Alai racketeering. Mark received a twenty year sentence with parole for the murder. Palmer had yet been arrested, one Summer Hill leader got caught and the other never will be.

It was difficult for me to take everything in as it all happened so fast. I could not do anything for my brother, other than what Palmer told me to do. Mark had fallen into place just as our father had. Neither had any control of their actions once a substance encouraged them.

Kenny and I continued living together, until Jai Alai was shut down. Kenny continued his entrepreneurial escapade until caught in 1985. I went back to Pittsfield and rebought the farm with my comfortable illegitimate earnings. Ski saved all his money from the boss after he saw what drug use and gambling did to Kenny. He got out of Jai Alai immediately after the fiasco. He then lived the American dream, collecting unemployment.

After Kenny got arrested in 1985, his philosophies on freedom and drugs had changed. He wrote me one final letter from prison before he died of pneumonia:

> Dear Pat,
>
> I ain't free no more. Yet strangely, I still have God, mainly, I think it is because of all my free time. I'm imprisoned for being a street pharmacist; all I did was simply sell an herb to make others happy. However, a federal agent got away with planning a murder and a President, who intentionally fought a war responsible for thirty thousand deaths, never had been viewed as deviant. All these acts were for individual prosperity, unlike my kind act. Consequently, I'm here rotting for five more years because of a drug as harmful as cigarettes.
>
> Pot makes me want to eat and sleep, not fight people as alcohol inevitably invites. Sharing a cultural act for many in America has gotten me enslaved, and now I am giving my employment

to the state for free. I get arrested for selling a drug celebrating happiness and intellect, yet rulers were provided through the extermination of peaceful cultures. "Our prejudices and passions have been used as the instruments of their subjection and slavery"[clxiii].

Just as the journal taught me, the considerate treatment offered by the Indians was denied. The words of Eluwilussit have inspired me thanks to your journal. It had become "doubtful that many of [the Indians] wanted to recapture their ancestors less sophisticated lifestyle. The European's were in America to stay. The only question was which Europeans the Indians had to deal with. If the French drove out the English, the Indians would have to make peace with the French"[clxiv].

Unlike the Europeans during 1812 who used immoral theory to capitalize on New England, God has put me in this place to help myself, so that I can help others. I now study the Bible as I once had history. I realize that all the murders and unfortunate events regarding Jai Alai have occurred due to the illegitimate acts made by the same politicians who justified the destructive expansion through God's will.

Unfortunately, the original theory of God's necessary expansion made original New Englanders ruthless to obtain wealth ruining any tranquility amongst natives. The Dark Ages destruction of philosophy came with the loss of free discussion. King Phillip's War had followed the Dark Ages, as with The War of 1812, which ignored the universal intellect, destroying civility throughout the American frontier.

Thus, Hartford was put in an impossible position to become a pleasant city, mainly due to the Hartford Convention's objection toward Madison's war. The city, as with us, had no choice but illegitimacy to achieve, because Hartford did not back unconstitutional acts during war. Madison had no problem sacrificing an army due to ignorance and lack of pity, which only was beneficial to the foreign conquerors and American expansionists.

If it had not been for the Convention, New England would have become under the rule of the Confederacy, as Madison's political allies planned with England. As inhabitants with hatred for New England spread through the Union, their representing politicians made sure to fracture Hartford and the opposing New Englanders.

Thank you so much Pat. Finally someone was able to share lost truths with me. You were taught the immorality used by some of the men who formed our justice, especially during the two expanding wars mentioned in your journal, which declined equal opportunity. The illegitimacy of the government's attempt to gain reign over New England by declaring an unprepared war had snowballed into a society in which rules have to be broken to succeed.

Illegitimacy in America's society had expanded during the civil war of King Phillips to the Civil War of America; It became a legislative practice as

Madison and his cabinet practiced warfare. Just as "James Monroe, Mr. Madison's secretary of state and William Pinkney, Mr. Madison's attorney general, did, while ministers at London, making an arrangement with the British government, on this very subject; and in their letter to Mr. Madison, insisted, that the arrangement so made by them, ought to be perfectly satisfactory"[clxv].

The militia by 1812 had become a "devouring monster that had to be fed, clothed, housed, and otherwise tended to; beyond the cost of the army itself were all the knavish charges of the numerous tribe of contractors. If statesman were better at arithmetic, wars would be far fewer. England might have purchased Canada from France for much less than England had paid to fight the war that won the province"[clxvi].

These avoidable trifles reflected "America's darker theme. It involved a lion, king of the beasts, who numbered among his subjects a body of faithful dogs, devoted to his person and government, and through whose assistance he had greatly extended his dominions. The lion, however, influenced by evil counselors, took an aversion to the dogs, condemned them unheard, and ordered his tigers, leopards, and panthers to attack and destroy them. The brave dogs, dismayed at their masters change of heart, reluctantly defended themselves but not without internal dissent. A few among them, of a mongrel race, derived from a mixture with wolves and foxes, corrupted by royal promises of great rewards,

deserted the honest dogs and joined their enemies. Horses and bulls, as well as dogs, might
thus be divided amongst their own kind, and
civil wars produced at pleasure. All would be
so weakened that neither liberty nor safety
would survive, and nothing would remain but
abject submission to a despot"[clxvii].

"As they enabled the king to reward killing, it
established a precedent that justified a tyrant to
make like promises; and every example of such an
unnatural brute rewarded additional strength"[clxviii].

I'm here for pot, yet Madison, who put a
country in jeopardy of losing its independence, was never apprehended. Simply and
sadly Pat, "The friends of war will never make
peace; that tree does not produce such fruit. If
we wish for peace, let us be reasonable; let the
friends of peace be employed to make it. We
must change our rulers; we must elect no
more such men as they are, and we shall again
be happy"[clxix].

Finally Pat, "Divine Providence has established"[clxx] no consistency amongst generations
which were driven by moral theory. We need to
find "a new world, in the sense, that so many of
us seem to have forgotten in this day of rocket
ships and atom bombs, that our last opportunity
for oncoming generations to create a society of
peace and harmony in a world of hate and suspicion, depends on the new world for the errant
children of a loving God"[clxxi]. The base of our
democracy had been cracked as a result of an
inconsistent opinion of justice. We can begin to

avoid any additional structure damage by eliminating falsehood. The truth will set us free.

Keep Breathing,
Kenny

Kenny died in prison, but not before I sent him a copy of this story.

Bibliography

Brands, H.W.*The First American: The Life and Times of Benjamin Franklin,* New York, Doubleday, 2000

Burpee, Charles W. *History of Hartford County Vol.1* Chicago, Hartford, Boston, The S. J. Clarke Publishing Company, 1928

Drake, James D. *King Phillip's War (Civil War in New England, 1675-1676),* Massachusetts, The University of Massachusetts Press, 1999

Dwight, Theodore *History of the Hartford Convention: With a Review of the Policy of the United States Government, which led to The War of 1812,* New York, Books for Libraries Press, 1833

Flint, Farris A. *The Pan American: Mexican Oil Refinery,* New York,The Famous Features Syndicate Inc., 1946.

Gardenier, Barent *The Examiner Vol. 1: Containing Political Essays on the Most Important Events of the time; Public Laws and Official Documents*, New York, Printed and Published by the Editor Barent Gardenier, 1814

Knowles, David *The Evolution of Medieval Thought,* Toronto, Random House of Canada Limited,1962

Lesser, David M. *No. 86 Rare America (A Catalogue of Significant and Unusual Imprints Relating to America)*, Connecticut, Lesser, 2005

Lesser, David M. *Number 91 Rare America: A Catalogue of Significant and Unusual Imprints Relating to America 2006)*, Lesser, CT

Madison, James *First Inauguration speech,* 1809

Mahony, Edmund H. *Hartford Courant: Former FBI Agent Indicted in Killing*, Connecticut, Hartford Courant, May 5, 2005

Steele, Joel Dorman & Esther Baker *Barnes Historical Series: A Brief History of the United States,* New York, Cincinatti, Chicago, A. S. Barnes & Company,1900

The First Charter of Virginia, April 10, 1606

Notes

i Dwight, pg. 28, 1833
ii Drake, Cover, 1999
iii Burpee, pg. 126, 1928
iv Burpee, pg. 126, 1928
v Steele, pg. 14, 1900
vi Hart, pg. 219, 1893
vii Steele, pg. 24, 1900
viii Steele, pg.25, 1900
ix Steele, pg. 25-26, 1900
x Steele, pg. 25, 1900
xi Steele, pg. 26, 1900
xii Steele, pg. 35
xiii Steele, pg. 46, 1900
xiv Drake, Cover, 1999
xv Drake, 199, 1999
xvi Drake, 27, 1999
xvii Drake, 27, 1999
xviii Drake, 27, 1999
xix Steele, pf. 57, 1900
xx Burpee, pg. 44, 1928
xxi Burpee, pg. 126-127, 1928
xxii Steele, pg. 57, 1900

xxiii Drake, pg. 89, 1999
xxiv Drake, pg. 171, 1999
xxv Gardenier, pg. 5, 1814
xxvi Gardenier, pg. 14, 1814
xxvii Gardenier, pg. 6, 1814
xxviii Gardenier, pg. 1, 1814
xxix Gardenier, pg. 1, 1814
xxx Gardeneir, pg. 7, 1814
xxxi Gardenier, pg. 13, 1814
xxxii Gardenier, pg. 6, 1814
xxxiii Gardenier, pg. 6, 1814
xxxiv Gardenier, pg. 6, 1814
xxxv Gardenier, pg. 19, 1814
xxxvi Drake, pg. 42, 1999
xxxvii Drake, pg. 28, 1999
xxxviii Burpee, pg. 45, 1927
xxxix Drake, pg. 28, 1999
xl Drake, pg. 29, 1999
xli Drake, pg. 29, 1999
xlii Drake, Pg.101, 1999
xliii Burpee, pg. 133, 1928
xliv Drake, Pg.58, 1999
xlv Burpee, pg. 131, 1928
xlvi Thwaites, pg. 170-171, 1894
xlvii Drake, Pg. 57, 1999
xlviii Steele, pg. 57-58, 1900
xlix Drake, pg. 115, 1999
l Drake, pg. 118, 1999
li Steele, pg. 58-59, 1900
lii Steele, pg. 58-59, 1900
liii Drake, pg. 119, 1999
liv Drake, pg. 120, 1999
lv Drake, pg. 58, 1900

[lvi] Thwaites, pg. 170, 1894

[lvii] Drake, 1999

[lviii] Drake, pg. 39, 1999

[lix] Drake, pg. 156, 1999

[lx] Drake, pg. 87, 1999

[lxi] Thwaites, pg. 172, 1894

[lxii] Drake, pg. 98, 1999

[lxiii] Drake, pg.173, 1999

[lxiv] Burpee, pg. 44, 1928

[lxv] Gardenier, pg.14, 1814

[lxvi] Gardenier, pg.15, 1814

[lxvii] Brands, pg. 693, 2000

[lxviii] Drake, pg. 171, 1999

[lxix] Drake, pg. 170, 1999

[lxx] Burpee, pg. 131, 1928

[lxxi] Drake, pg. 117, 1999

[lxxii] Burpee, pg. 127, 1928

[lxxiii] Drake, pg. 97, 1999

[lxxiv] Drake, pg. 156, 1999

[lxxv] Drake, pg. 156, 1999

[lxxvi] Barnes, pg. 59, 1900

[lxxvii] Barnes, pg. 59, 1900

[lxxviii] Barnes, pg. 59, 1900

[lxxix] Drake, pg. 156 1900

[lxxx] Barnes, pg. 158, 1900

[lxxxi] Barnes, pg. 61, 1900

[lxxxii] Barnes, pg. 92, 1900

[lxxxiii] Hart, pg. 208, 1893

[lxxxiv] Barnes, pg. 90, 1900

[lxxxv] Barnes, pg. 163 1900

[lxxxvi] Barnes, pg. 158, 1900

[lxxxvii] Barnes, 161, 1900

[lxxxviii] Hart, pg. 212, 1893

lxxxix Hart, pg 215, 1893

xc Gardenier, pg. 54, 1814

xci Gardenier, pg. 98, 1814

xcii Hart, Pg. 157, 1893

xciii Burpee, pg. 272, 1928

xciv Burpee, pg. 272, 1928

xcv Barnes, pg. 161, 1900

xcvi Hart, pg. 209, 1893

xcvii Burpee, pg. 273, 1928

xcviii Burpee, pg. 272, 1928

xcix Barnes, pg. 160, 1900

c Barnes, pg.160, 1900

ci Gardenier, pg. 401-411, 1814

cii Hart, pg. 209, 1893

ciii Hart, pg. 212, 1893

civ Gardenier, pg. 197, 1814

cv Barnes, pg. 165, 1900

cvi Barnes, pg. 165, 1900

cvii Gardenier, pg. 330, 1814

cviii Hart, pg. 212- 213, 1893

cix Hart, pg. 203, 1893

cx Gardenier, pg.97, 1814

cxi Gardenier, pg. 97, 1814

cxii Gardenier, pg. 159, 1814

cxiii Gardenier, pg. 169, 1814

cxiv Gardenier, pg.169, 1814

cxv Barnes, pg. 50, 1900

cxvi Lesser, Entry #58, 2005

cxvii Thwaites, pg. 182, 1894

cxviii Gardenier, pg. 12, 1814

cxix Madison, First Inauguration, 1809

cxx Hart, Pg. 160-161, 1893

cxxi Hart, pg.212, 1893

cxxii Dwight, pg. 13, 1833

cxxiii Gardenier, pg. 372, 1814

cxxiv Hart, pg. 220, 1893

cxxv Barnes, pg. 169, 1900

cxxvi Gardenier, Pg. 72, 1814

cxxvii Gardenier, Pg. 34, 1814

cxxviii Gardenier, pg.107, 1814

cxxix Gardenier, pg. 372, 1814

cxxx Gardenier, pg. 138, 1814

cxxxi Gardenier, pg. 171, 1814

cxxxii Gardenier, pg. 180, 1814.

cxxxiii Burpee, pg. 275, 1928

cxxxiv Burpee, pg. 275, 1928

cxxxv Burpee, pg. 275, 1928

cxxxvi Gardenier, pg. 259, 1814

cxxxvii Gardenier, pg. 192, 1814

cxxxviii Hart, pg. 220, 1893

cxxxix Gardenier, pg. 415, 1814

cxl Hart, pg. 214, 1893

cxli Gardenier, pg. 415, 1814

cxlii Hart, pg. 215, 1893

cxliii Hart, pg. 215

cxliv Gardenier, pg. 73, 1814

cxlv Gardenier, pg. 73, 1814

cxlvi Hart, pg. 206, 1893

cxlvii Hart, pg. 208, 1893

cxlviii Lesser, #2, 2006

cxlix Gardenier, pg. 289, 1814

cl The First Charter of Virginia, 1606

cli Knowles, pg. 36, 1962

clii Gardenier, pg. 302, 1814

cliii Knowles, pg. 32, 1962

cliv Knowles, pg. 49, 1962

clv Knowles, Pg. 42-49, 1962

clvi Mahoney, A1, 2005

clvii Mahoney, A1, 2005

clviii Mahoney, A1, 2005

clix Mahoney, A1, 2005

clx Mahoney, A1, 2005

clxi Mahoney, A1, 2005

clxii Mahoney, A1, 2005

clxiii Gardenier, pg. 394, 1814

clxiv Brands, pg. 267, 2000

clxv Gardenier, pg. 83, 1814

clxvi Brands, pg. 640, 2000

clxvii Brands, pg. 643-644, 2000

clxviii Brands, pg. 644, 2000

clxix Gardenier, pg. 83, 1814

clxx Gardenier, pg. 168, 1814

clxxi Flint, Back Cover, 1946